glencoe

teenhealth

building healthy relationships

Mc
Graw
Hill
Education

Bothell, WA • Chicago, IL • Columbus, OH • New York, NY

Meet the Authors

Mary H. Bronson, Ph.D. recently retired after teaching for 30 years in Texas public schools. Dr. Bronson taught health education in grades K–12 as well as health education methods classes at the graduate and undergraduate levels. As Health Education Specialist for the Dallas School District, Dr. Bronson developed and implemented a district-wide health eduation program. She has been honored as Texas Health Educator of the Year by the Texas Association for Health, Physical Education, Recreation, and Dance and selected Teacher of the Year twice by her colleagues. Dr. Bronson has assisted school districts throughout the country in developing local health education programs. She is also the coauthor of Glencoe Health.

Michael J. Cleary, Ed.D., C.H.E.S. is a professor at Slippery Rock University, where he teaches methods courses and supervises field experiences. Dr. Cleary taught health education at Evanston Township High School in Illinois and later served as the Lead Teacher Specialist at the McMillen Center for Health Education in Fort Wayne, Indiana. Dr. Cleary has published widely on curriculum development and assessment in K–12 and college health education. Dr. Cleary is also coauthor of Glencoe Health.

Betty M. Hubbard, Ed.D., C.H.E.S. has taught science and health education in grades 6–12 as well as undergraduate- and graduate-level courses. She is a professor at the University of Central Arkansas, where in addition to teaching she conducts in-service training for health education teachers in school districts throughout Arkansas. In 1991, Dr. Hubbard received the university's teaching excellence award. Her publications, grants, and presentations focus on research-based, comprehensive health instruction. Dr. Hubbard is a fellow of the American Association for Health Education and serves as the contributing editor of the Teaching Ideas feature of the American Journal of Health Education.

Contributing Author

Dinah Zike, M.Ed. is an international curriculum consultant and inventor who has designed and developed educational products and three-dimensional, interactive graphic organizers for more than 35 years. As president and founder of Dinah-Might Adventures, L.P., Dinah is author of more than 100 award-winning educational publications. Dinah has a B.S. and an M.S. in educational curriculum and instruction from Texas A&M University. Dinah Zike's Foldables® are an exclusive feature of McGraw-Hill.

MHEonline.com

Send all inquiries to:
McGraw-Hill Education
STEM Learning Solutions Center
8787 Orion Place
Columbus, OH 43240

ISBN: 978-0-07-664050-8
MHID: 0-07-664050-7

Printed in the United States of America.

5 6 7 8 9 LMN 22 21 20 19 18

STEM McGraw-Hill is committed to providing instructional materials in Science, Technology, Engineering, and Mathematics (STEM) that give all students a solid foundation, one that prepares them for college and careers in the 21st century.

Reviewers

Professional Reviewers

Amy Eyler, Ph.D., CHES
Washington University in St. Louis
St. Louis, Missouri

Shonali Saha, M.D.
Johns Hopkins School of Medicine
Baltimore, Maryland

Roberta Duyff
Duyff & Associates
St. Louis, MO

Teacher Reviewers

Lou Ann Donlan
Altoona Area School District
Altoona, PA

Steve Federman
Loveland Intermediate School
Loveland, Ohio

Rick R. Gough
Ashland Middle School
Ashland, Ohio

Jacob Graham
Oblock Junior High
Plum, Pennsylvania

William T. Gunther
Clarkston Community Schools
Clarkston, MI

Ellie Hancock
Somerset Area School District
Somerset, PA

Diane Hursky
Independence Middle School
Bethel Park, PA

Veronique Javier
Thomas Cardoza Middle School
Jackson, Mississippi

Patricia A. Landon
Patrick F. Healy Middle School
East Orange, NJ

Elizabeth Potash
Council Rock High School South
Holland, PA

The Path to Good Health

Your health book has many features that will aid you in your learning. Some of these features are listed below. You can use the map at the right to help you find these and other special features in the book.

* The **Big Idea** can be found at the start of each lesson.

* Your **Foldables®** help you organize your notes.

* The **Quick Write** at the start of each lesson will help you think about the topic and give you an opportunity to write about it in your journal.

* The **Bilingual Glossary** contains vocabulary terms and definitions in Spanish and English.

* **Health Skills Activities** help you learn more about each of the 10 health skills.

* **Infographs** provide a colorful, visual way to learn about current health news and trends.

* The **Fitness Zone** provides an online fitness resource that includes podcasts, videos, activity cards, and more!

* **Hands-On Health Activities** give you the opportunity to complete hands-on projects.

* **Videos** encourage you to explore real life health topics.

* **Audio** directs you to online audio chapter summaries.

* **Web Quest** activities challenge you to relate lesson concepts to current health news and research.

* **Review** your understanding of health concepts with lesson reviews and quizzes.

What's the word on the street? The **glossary** lists vocabulary terms in English and Spanish.

Quick! Write about your good health habits using a **Quick Write** activity.

Think big! Start your journey with a **Big Idea** and increase your pace with **Foldables®**.

Sharpen your skills with **Health Skills Activities**.

Got a nose for news? Check out each chapter's **infographs** for health news and trends.

Get into the zone –the **Fitness Zone!** Listen to podcasts, watch videos, and more.

Show what you know by completing a **Hands-On Health Activity**.

Stop! Look and Listen! Watch a Health eSpotlight **video** and explore real life health topics. Listen to the **audio** summaries to review the chapter.

Go on a quest. Take a **Web Quest** to learn more about health news and research.

Finish strong! **Review** your understanding of health concepts with lesson reviews and quizzes.

Contents

F4F-1 through F4F-9
Flip your book over to see a special section on fitness.

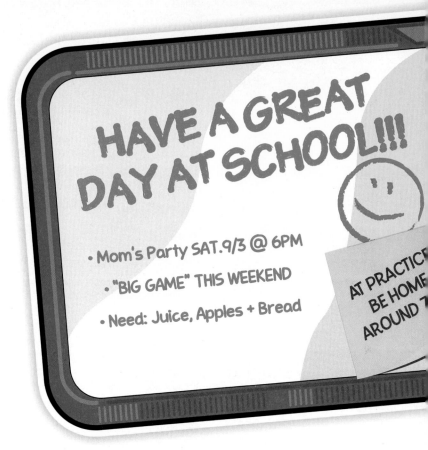

chapter

1 Building Healthy Relationships

chapter 2 | Dating Relationships + Abstinence

Your Total Health

WHAT IS HEALTH?

Do you know someone you would describe as "healthy"? What kinds of traits do they have? Maybe they are involved in sports. Maybe they just "look" healthy. Looking fit and feeling well are important, but there is more to having good health. Good health also includes getting along well with others and feeling good about yourself.

Your **physical**, **emotional**, and **social** *health* are all **related** and make up your *total* **health.**

Health, the *combination of physical, mental/emotional, and social well-being,* may look like the sides of a triangle. You need all three sides to make the triangle. Each side supports the other two sides. Your physical health, mental/emotional health, and social health are all related and make up your total health.

Physical Health

Physical health is one side of the health triangle. Engaging in physical activity every day will help to build and maintain your physical health. Some of the ways you can improve your physical health include the following:

> ✳ **EATING HEALTHY FOODS** Choose nutritious meals and snacks.
>
> ✳ **VISITING THE DOCTOR REGULARLY** Get regular checkups from a doctor and a dentist.
>
> ✳ **CARING FOR PERSONAL HYGIENE** Shower or bathe each day. Brush and floss your teeth at least twice every day.
>
> ✳ **WEARING PROTECTIVE GEAR** When playing sports, using protective gear and following safety rules will help you avoid injuries.
>
> ✳ **GET ENOUGH SLEEP** Most teens need about nine hours of sleep every night.

You can also have good physical health by avoiding harmful behaviors, such as using alcohol, tobacco, and other drugs. The use of tobacco has been linked to many diseases, such as heart disease and cancer.

Mental/Emotional Health

Another side of the health triangle is your mental/emotional health. How do you handle your feelings, thoughts, and emotions each day? You can improve your mental/emotional health by talking and thinking about yourself in a healthful way. Share your thoughts and feelings with your family, a trusted adult, or with a friend.

If you are mentally and emotionally healthy, you can face challenges in a positive way. Be patient with yourself when you try to learn new subjects or new skills. Remember that everybody makes mistakes—including you! Next time you can do better.

Taking action to reach your goals is another way to develop good mental/emotional health. This can help you focus your energy and give you a sense of accomplishment. Make healthful choices, keep your promises, and take responsibility for what you do, and you will feel good about yourself and your life.

Social Health

A third side of the health triangle is your social health. Social health means how you relate to people at home, at school, and everywhere in your world. Strong friendships and family relationships are signs of good social health.

Do you get along well with your friends, classmates, and teachers? Do you spend time with your family? You can develop skills for having good relationships. Good social health includes supporting the people you care about. It also includes communicating with, respecting, and valuing people. Sometimes you may disagree with others. You can disagree and express your thoughts, but be thoughtful and choose your words carefully.

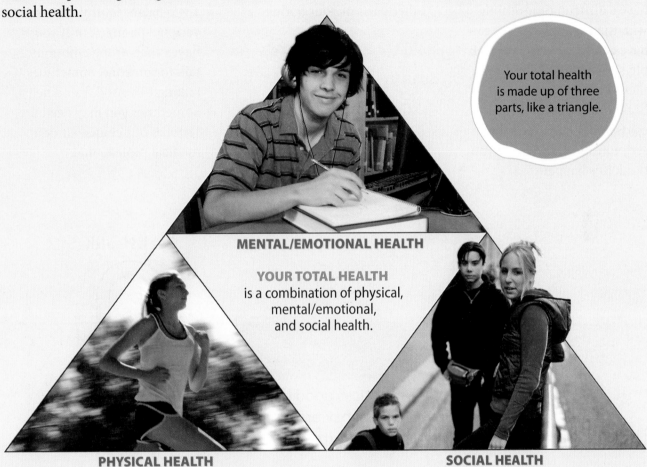

Your total health is made up of three parts, like a triangle.

MENTAL/EMOTIONAL HEALTH

YOUR TOTAL HEALTH is a combination of physical, mental/emotional, and social health.

PHYSICAL HEALTH

SOCIAL HEALTH

ACHIEVING WELLNESS

What is the difference between health and wellness? Wellness is *a state of well-being or balanced health over a long period of time.* Your health changes from day to day. One day you may feel tired if you did not get enough sleep. Maybe you worked very hard at sports practice. The next day, you might feel well rested and full of energy because you rested. Your emotions also change. You might feel sad one day but happy the next day.

Your overall health is like a snapshot of your physical, mental/emotional, and social health. Your wellness takes a longer view. Being healthy means balancing the three sides of your health triangle over weeks or months. Wellness is sometimes represented by a continuum, or scale, that gives a picture of your health at a certain time. It may also tell you how well you are taking care of yourself.

The Mind-Body Connection

Your emotions have a lot to do with your physical health. Think about an event in your own life that made you feel sad. How did you deal with this emotion? Sometimes people have a difficult time dealing with their emotions. This can have a negative effect on their physical health. For example, they might get headaches, backaches, upset stomachs, colds, the flu, or even more serious diseases. Why do you think this happens?

Your mind and body connect through your nervous system. This system includes thousands of miles of nerves. The nerves link your brain to your body. Upsetting thoughts and feelings sometimes affect the signals from your brain to other parts of your body.

Your **emotions** have *a lot* to do with *your* **physical health.**

The mind-body connection describes *how your emotions affect your physical and overall health and how your overall health affects your emotions.* This connection shows again how important it is to keep the three sides of the health triangle balanced. If you become very sad or angry, or if you have other strong emotions, talk to someone. Sometimes talking to a good friend helps. Sometimes you may need the services of a counselor or a medical professional.

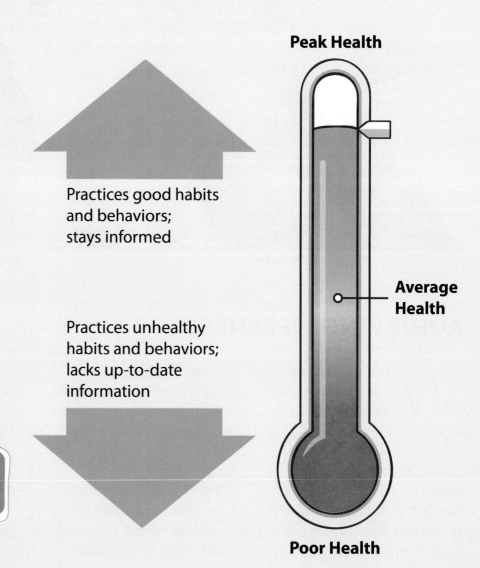

Practices good habits and behaviors; stays informed

Practices unhealthy habits and behaviors; lacks up-to-date information

The Wellness Scale identifies how healthy you are at a given point in time.

Peak Health

Average Health

Poor Health

Health Influences *and* Risk Factors

WHAT INFLUENCES YOUR HEALTH?

What are your favorite foods or activities? Your answers reflect your personal tastes, or likes and dislikes. Your health is influenced by your personal tastes and by many other factors such as:

- heredity
- environment
- family and friends
- culture
- media
- attitudes
- behavior

Heredity

You can control some of these factors, but not all of them. For example, you cannot control the natural color of your hair or eyes. **Heredity** (huh•RED•i•tee) is *the passing of traits from parents to their biological children.* Heredity determines the color of your eyes and hair, and other physical traits, or parts of your appearance. Genes are the basic units of heredity. They are made from chemicals called DNA, and they create the pattern for your physical traits. You inherited, or received, half of your DNA from your mother and half from your father.

Traits such as eye and hair color are inherited from parents.

Environment

Think about where you live. Do you live in a city, a suburb, a small town, or in a rural area? Where you live is the physical part of your **environment** (en•VY•ruhn•mehnt), or *all the living and nonliving things around you.*

Environment is another factor that affects your personal health. Your physical environment includes the home you live in, the school you attend, and the air and water around you.

Your *social environment* includes the people in your life. They can be friends, classmates, and neighbors. Your friends and **peers,** or *people close to you in age who are a lot like you,* may influence your choices.

You may feel pressure to think and act like them. Peer pressure can also influence health choices. The influence can be positive or negative. Helping a friend with homework, volunteering with a friend, or simply listening to a friend are examples of positive peer influence. A friend who wants you to drink alcohol, for example, is a negative influence. Recreation is also a part of your social environment. Playing games and enjoying physical activities with others can have a positive effect on your health.

Culture

Your family is one of the biggest influences on your life. It shapes your <u>cultural background,</u> or *the beliefs, customs, and traditions of a specific group of people.* You learned that your family influences your health. In addition to your family, your <u>culture,</u> or *the collected beliefs, customs, and behaviors of a group,* also affects your health. Your family and their culture may influence the foods you eat as well as the activities and special events you celebrate with special foods. Some families fast (do not eat food) during religious events. Ahmed's family observes the holiday of Ramadan.

During this holiday, members of his family fast until sundown. Your family might also celebrate traditions that include dances, foods, ceremonies, songs, and games. Your culture can also affect your health. Knowing how your lifestyle and family history relate to health problems can help you stay well.

Media

What do television, radio, movies, magazines, newspapers, books, billboards, and the Internet have in common? They are all forms of <u>media,</u> or *various methods for communicating information.* The media is another factor that affects your personal health.

The media provide powerful sources of information and influence.

You may learn helpful new facts about health on the Internet or television. You might also see a commercial for the latest video game or athletic shoes. The goal of commercials on television or the Internet, as well as advertisements in print, is to make you want to buy a product. The product may be good or bad for your health. You can make wise health choices by learning to <u>evaluate,</u> or *determine the quality* of everything you see, hear, or read.

The celebration of Kwanzaa is a tradition in many African American families.

YOUR BEHAVIOR AND YOUR HEALTH

Do you protect your skin from the sun? Do you get enough sleep so that you are not tired during the day? Do you eat healthful foods? Do you listen to a friend who needs to talk about a problem? Your answers to these questions reflect your personal lifestyle factors, or *the behaviors and habits that help determine a person's level of health.* Positive lifestyle factors promote good health. Negative lifestyle factors promote poor health.

Positive lifestyle factors promote **good** health.

Your attitude, or your *feelings and beliefs,* toward your personal lifestyle factors plays an important role in your health. You will also have greater success in managing your health if you keep a positive attitude. Teens who have a positive attitude about their health are more likely to practice good health habits and take responsibility for their health.

Risk Behaviors

"Dangerous intersection. Proceed with caution." "Don't walk." "No lifeguard on duty." You have probably seen these signs or similar signs. They are posted to warn you about possible risks or dangers and to keep you safe.

Eating well-balanced meals, starting with a good breakfast.

Getting at least 60 minutes of physical activity daily.

Sleeping at least eight hours every night.

Doing your best in school and other activities.

Avoiding tobacco, alcohol, and other drugs.

Following safety rules and wearing protective gear.

Relating well to family, friends, and classmates.

Lifestyle factors affect your personal health.

Risk, or *the chance that something harmful may happen to your health and wellness,* is part of everyday life. Some risks are easy to identify. Everyday tasks such as preparing food with a knife or crossing a busy street both carry some risk. Other risks are more hidden. Some foods you like might be high in fat.

You cannot avoid every kind of risk. However, the risks you can avoid often involve risk behavior. A risk behavior is an action or behavior that might cause injury or harm to you or others. Playing a sport can be risky, but if you wear protective gear, you may avoid injury. Wear a helmet when you ride a bike to avoid the risk of a head injury if you fall. Smoking cigarettes is another risk behavior that you can avoid. Riding in a car without a safety belt is a risk behavior you can avoid by buckling up. Another risk behavior is having a lifestyle with little physical activity, such as sitting in front of the TV or a computer instead of being active. You can avoid many kinds of risk by taking responsibility for your personal health behaviors and avoiding risk.

RISKS AND CONSEQUENCES

All risk behaviors have consequences. Some consequences are minor or short-term. You might eat a sweet snack just before dinner so that you lose your appetite for a healthy meal. Other risk behaviors may have serious or life-threatening consequences. These are long-term consequences.

Experimenting with alcohol, tobacco, or other drugs has long-term consequences that can seriously damage your health. They can affect all three sides of your health triangle. They can lead to dangerous addictions, which are physical and mental dependencies.

These substances can confuse the user's judgment and can increase the risks he or she takes. Using these substances may also lead to problems with family and friends, and problems at school.

Risks that affect your health are more complicated when they are **cumulative risks** (KYOO•myuh•luh•tiv), which occur *when one risk factor adds to another to increase danger.* For example, making unhealthy food choices is one risk. Not getting regular physical activity is another risk. Add these two risks together over time, and you raise your risk of developing diseases such as heart disease and cancer.

Many choices you make affect your health. Knowing the consequences of your choices and behaviors can help you take responsibility for your health.

Reducing Risks

Practicing **prevention,** *taking steps to avoid something,* is the best way to deal with risks. For example, wear a helmet when you ride a bike to help prevent head injury. Slow down when walking or running on wet or icy pavement to help prevent a fall. Prevention also means watching out for possible dangers. When you know dangers are ahead, you can avoid them and prevent accidents.

Physical injury can be a consequence of risk behaviors.

EHproductions Ltd/Blend Images LLC

STAYING INFORMED You can take responsibility for your health by staying informed. Learn about developments in health to maintain your own health. Getting a physical exam at least once a year by a doctor is another way to stay informed about your health.

CHOOSING ABSTINENCE
If you practice abstinence from risk behaviors, you care for your own health and others' health by preventing illness and injury. Abstinence is *the conscious, active choice not to participate in high-risk behaviors.* By choosing not to use tobacco, you may avoid getting lung cancer. By staying away from alcohol, illegal drugs, and sexual activity, you avoid the negative consequences of these risk behaviors.

Abstinence is good for all sides of your health triangle. It promotes your physical health by helping you avoid injury and illness. It protects your mental/emotional health by giving you peace of mind. It also benefits your relationships with family members, peers, and friends. Practicing abstinence shows you are taking responsibility for your personal health behaviors and that you respect yourself and others. You can feel good about making positive health choices, which will strengthen your mental/emotional health as well as your social health.

✓ Plan ahead.

✓ Think about consequences.

✓ Resist negative pressure from others.

✓ Stay away from risk takers.

✓ Pay attention to what you are doing.

✓ Know your limits.

✓ Be aware of dangers.

Reducing risk behaviors will help maintain your overall health.

Getting regular checkups is one form of prevention.

XV

Building Health Skills

SKILLS FOR A HEALTHY LIFE

Health skills are *skills that help you become and stay healthy.* Health skills can help you improve your physical, mental/emotional, and social health. Just as you learn math, reading, sports, and other kinds of skills, you can learn skills for taking care of your health now and for your entire life.

These ten skills affect your physical, mental/emotional, and social health and can benefit you throughout your life.

Health Skills	What It Means to You
Accessing Information	You know how to find valid and reliable health information and health-promoting products and services.
Practicing Healthful Behaviors	You take action to reduce risks and protect yourself against illness and injury.
Stress Management	You find healthy ways to reduce and manage stress in your life.
Analyzing Influences	You recognize the many factors that influence your health, including culture, media, and technology.
Communication Skills	You express your ideas and feelings and listen when others express theirs.
Refusal Skills	You can say no to risky behaviors.
Conflict-Resolution Skills	You can work out problems with others in healthful ways.
Decision Making	You think through problems and find healthy solutions.
Goal Setting	You plan for the future and work to make your plans come true.
Advocacy	You take a stand for the common good and make a difference in your home, school, and community.

SELF-MANAGEMENT SKILLS

When you were younger, your parents and other adults decided what was best for your health. Now that you are older, you make many of these decisions for yourself. You take care of your personal health. You are developing your self-management skills. Two key self-management skills are practicing healthful behaviors and managing stress. When you eat healthy foods and get enough sleep, you are taking actions that promote good health. Stress management is learning to cope with challenges that put a strain on you mentally or emotionally.

Practicing Healthful Behaviors

Your behaviors affect your physical, mental/emotional, and social health. You will see benefits quickly when you practice healthful behaviors. If you exercise regularly, your heart and muscles grow stronger. When you eat healthful foods and drink plenty of water, your body works well.

Getting a good night's sleep will help you wake up with more energy. Respecting and caring for others will help you develop healthy relationships. Managing your feelings in positive ways will help you avoid actions you may regret later.

Staying **positive** is a **good health** *habit.*

Practicing healthful behaviors can help prevent injury, illness, and other health problems. When you practice healthful actions, you can help your total health. Your total health means your physical, mental/emotional, and social health. This means you take care of yourself and do not take risks. It means you learn health-promoting habits. When you eat well-balanced meals and

healthful snacks and get regular physical checkups you are practicing good health habits. Staying positive is another good health habit.

Managing Stress

Learning ways to deal with stress, *the body's response to real or imagined dangers or other life events,* is an important self-management skill. Stress management can help you learn ways to deal with stress. Stress management means identifying sources of stress. It also means you learn how to handle stress in ways that support good health. Relaxation is a good way to deal with stress. Exercise is another way to positively deal with stress.

Studying for a test can cause stress.

Making Decisions *and* Setting Goals

The path to good health begins with making good decisions. You may make more of your own decisions now. Some of those decisions might be deciding which clothes to buy or which classes to take.

As you grow older, you gain more freedom, but with it comes more responsibility. You will need to understand the short-term and long-term consequences of decisions.

Another responsibility is goal setting. You also need to plan how to reach those goals.

When you learn how to set realistic goals, you take a step toward health and well-being. Learning to make decisions and to set goals will help give you purpose and direction in your life.

ACCESSING INFORMATION

Knowing how to get reliable, or *trust-worthy and dependable,* health information is an important skill. Where can you find all this information? A main source is from adults you can trust. Community resources give you other ways to get information. These include the library and government health agencies. Organizations such as the American Red Cross can also provide good information.

Reliable Sources

You can find facts about health and health-enhancing products or services through media sources such as television, radio, and the Internet. TV and radio interviews with health professionals can give you information about current scientific studies related to health.

Web sites that end in .gov and .edu are often the most reliable sites. These sites are maintained by government organizations and educational institutions.

Getting health information is important, but so is analyzing whether that health information is valid, or reliable. Carefully review web sites ending in .org.

Many of these sites are maintained by organizations, such as the American Cancer Society or American Diabetes Association. However, some sites ending in .org may not be legitimate.

The Internet can be a good source of health information.

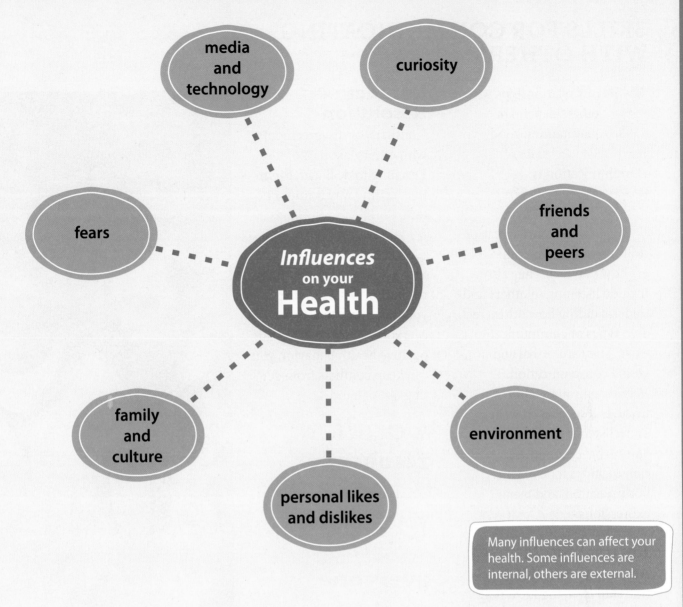

media
and
technology

curiosity

fears

Influences
on your
Health

friends
and
peers

family
and
culture

environment

personal likes
and dislikes

Many influences can affect your
health. Some influences are
internal, others are external.

Analyzing Influences

Learning how to analyze health information, products, and services will help you act in ways that protect your health. The first step in analyzing an influence is to identify its source. A TV commercial may tell you a certain food has health benefits.

Your **decisions** have to do with your *own* **values** and **beliefs**.

Ask yourself who is the source of the information. Next, think about the motive, or reason, for the influence. Does the advertiser really take your well-being into consideration? Does the ad make you curious about the product?

Does it try to scare you into buying the product? Analyzing influences involves recognizing factors that affect or influence your health.

Your decisions also have to do with your own values and beliefs. The opinions of your friends and family members affect your decisions. Your culture and messages from the media also affect your decisions.

SKILLS FOR COMMUNICATING WITH OTHERS

Your relationships with others depend on maintaining good communication skills. Communication is *the exchange of information through the use of words or actions.* Good communication skills include telling others how you feel. They also include listening to others and understanding how others feel. Two types of communication exist. They are verbal and nonverbal communication. Verbal communication involves a speaker or writer, and a listener or reader. Nonverbal communication includes tone of voice, body position, and using expressions.

Refusal Skills

An important communication skill is saying no. It may be something that is wrong. It may be something that you are not comfortable doing. You may worry what will happen if you don't go along with the group. Will your friends still like you? Will you still be a part of the group? It is at these times that refusal skills, or *strategies that help you say no effectively,* can help. Using refusal skills can sometimes be challenging, but they can help you stay true to yourself and to your beliefs. Also, other people will have respect for you for being honest.

Conflict Resolution

Conflicts, or disagreements with others, are part of life. Learning to deal with them in a healthy way is important. Conflict resolution is *a life skill that involves solving a disagreement in a way that satisfies both sides.* Conflict-resolution skills can help you find a way to satisfy everyone. Also, by using this positive health behavior, you can keep conflicts from getting out of hand.

Conflict **resolution** skills can help you find a way to *satisfy* **everyone.**

Advocacy

People with advocacy skills *take action in support of a cause.* They work to bring about a change by speaking out for something like health and wellness. When you speak out for health, you encourage other people to live healthy lives. Advocacy also means keeping others informed.

Using refusal skills effectively can help you avoid potentially dangerous situation.

Image Source/Getty Images

Making Decisions *and* Setting Goals

DECISIONS AND YOUR HEALTH

As you grow up, you usually gain more privileges. Along with privileges comes responsibility. You will make more of your own decisions. The choices and decisions you make can affect each part of your health triangle.

As you get older, you will learn to make more important decisions. You will need to understand the short-term and long-term consequences of the decisions you make.

You can learn the skill of making good decisions.

Some decisions may help you avoid harmful behaviors. These questions can help you understand some of the consequences of health-related decisions.

- How will this decision affect my health?
- Will it affect the health of others? If so, how?
- Is the behavior I might choose harmful or illegal?
- How will my family feel about my decision?
- Does this decision fit with my values?
- How will this decision affect my goals?

THE DECISION-MAKING PROCESS

You make decisions every day. Some decisions are easy to make. Other decisions are more difficult. Understanding the process of decision making, or *the process of making a choice or solving a problem,* will help you make the best possible decisions. The decision-making process can be broken down into six steps. You can apply these six steps to any decision you need to make.

Step 1: State the Situation

Identify the situation as you understand it. When you understand the situation and your choices you can make a sound decision. Ask yourself: What choice do you need to make? What are the facts? Who else is involved?

Step 2: List the Options

When you feel like you understand your situation, think of your options. List all of the possibilities you can think of. Be sure to include only those options that are safe. It is also important to ask an adult you trust for advice when making an important decision.

Step 3: Weigh the Possible Outcomes

After listing your options, you need to evaluate the consequences of each option. The word H.E.L.P. can be used to work through this step of the decision-making process.

- **H** (Healthful) What health risks will this option present to me and to others?
- **E** (Ethical) Does this choice reflect what my family and I believe to be ethical, or right? Does this choice show respect for me and others?
- **L** (Legal) Will I be breaking the law? Is this legal for someone my age?
- **P** (Parent Approval) Would my parents approve of this choice?

Step 4: Consider Your Values

Always consider your values or the beliefs that guide the way you live. Your values reflect what is important to you and what you have learned is right and wrong. Honesty, respect, consideration, and good health are values.

Step 5: Make a Decision and Act

You've weighed your options. You've considered the risks and consequences. Now you're ready for action. Choose the option that seems best for you. Remember that this step is not complete until you take action.

Step 6: Evaluate the Decision

Evaluating the results can help you make better decisions in the future. To evaluate the results, ask yourself: Was the outcome positive or negative? Were there any unexpected outcomes? Was there anything you could have done differently? How did your decision affect others? Do you think you made the right decision? What have you learned from the experience? If the outcome was not what you expected, try again.

Understanding the decision-making process will help you make sound decisions.

Step 1
State the situation.

Step 2
List the options.

Step 3
Weigh the possible outcomes.

Step 4
Consider your values.

Step 5
Make a decision and act.

Step 6
Evaluate the decision.

SETTING REALISTIC GOALS

When you think about your future, what do you see? Do you see someone who has graduated from college and has a good job? Are there things you want to achieve? Answering these questions can give you an idea of your goals in life. A goal is something you want to accomplish.

Goal setting is *the process of working toward something you want to accomplish.* When you have learned to set realistic goals, they can help you focus on what you want to accomplish in life. Realistic goals are goals you can reach.

Setting goals can benefit your health. Many goals can help to improve your overall health. Think about all you want to accomplish in life. Do you need to set some health-related goals to be able to accomplish those things?

Goals can become milestones and can tell you how far you have come. Reaching goals can be a powerful boost to your self-confidence. Improving your self-confidence can help to strengthen your mental/emotional health.

Types of Goals

There are two basic types of goals—short-term goals, *goals that you can achieve in a short length of time,* and long-term goals, *goals that you plan to reach over an extended period of time.* As the names imply, short-term goals can be accomplished more quickly than long-term goals.

Reaching *goals* can be a **powerful** *boost* to your **self confidence.**

Getting your homework turned in on time might be a short-term goal. Long-term goals are generally accomplished over months or years. Getting a college education might be a long-term goal. Often long-term goals are made up of short-term goals.

Reaching Your Goals

To accomplish your short-term and long-term goals, you need a plan. A goal-setting plan that has a series of steps for you to take can be very effective in helping you accomplish your goals. Following a plan can help you make the best use of your time, energy, and other resources. Here are the steps of a goal-setting plan:

- Step 1: Identify a specific goal and write it down. Write down exactly what your goal is. Be sure the goal is realistic.
- Step 2: List the steps to reach your goal. Breaking big goals into smaller goals can make them easier to accomplish.
- Step 3: Get help and support from others. There are many people in your life who can help you reach your goals. They may be parents, teachers, coaches, or other trusted adults.
- Step 4: Evaluate your progress. Check periodically to see if you are actually progressing toward your goal. You may have to identify and consider how to overcome an obstacle before moving toward your goal.
- Step 5: Celebrate when you reach your goal. Give yourself a reward.

Jamie has set a goal to be chosen for the all-star team

Choosing Health Services

WHAT IS HEALTH CARE?

You will probably at some point need to seek health care services. Health care provides services that promote, maintain, or restore health to individuals or communities. The health care system is all the medical care available to a nation's people, the way they receive the care, and the way the care is paid for. It is through the health care system that people receive medical services.

← Emergency

©Royalty-Free/Corbis

HEALTH CARE PROVIDERS

Many different professionals can help you with your health care. You may be most familiar with your own doctor who is your primary care provider: a health care professional who provides checkups and general care. Nurse practitioners and physician's assistants can also provide primary care.

In addition to doctors, nurse practitioners, and physician's assistants, many other health care professionals provide care. Nurses, pharmacists, health educators, counselors, mental health specialists, dentists, and nutritionists are all health care providers.

Preventive Care

Getting regular checkups is one way to prevent health problems and maintain wellness. During a checkup, your health care provider will check you carefully. She or he will check your heart and lungs and vision and hearing. You may also receive any immunizations you need. During your visit, your doctor may talk to you about healthful eating, exercise, avoiding alcohol, tobacco, and drugs, and other types of preventive care, or steps taken to keep disease or injury from happening or getting worse.

Specialists

Sometimes your primary care provider is not able to help you. In that case, he or she will refer you to a specialist, or health care professional trained to treat a special category of patients or specific health problems. Some specialists treat specific types of people. Other specialists treat specific conditions or body systems.

Different specialists treat different conditions.

Specialist	Specialty
Allergist	Asthma, hay fever, other allergies
Cardiologist	Heart problems
Dermatologist	Skin conditions and diseases
Oncologist	Cancer
Ophthalmologist	Eye diseases
Orthodontist	Tooth and jaw irregularities
Orthopedist	Broken bones and similar problems
Otolaryngologist	Ear, nose, and throat
Pediatrician	Infants, children, and teens

HEALTH CARE SETTINGS

Years ago, people were very limited as to where they could go for health care. In more recent years, new types of health care delivery settings have been developed. People now can go to their doctors' offices, hospitals, surgery centers, hospices, and assisted living communities.

Doctors' Offices

Doctors' offices are probably the most common setting for receiving health care. Your doctor, nurse practitioner, or physician's assistant has medical equipment to help them diagnose illnesses and to give checkups. Most of your medical needs can be met at your doctor's office.

Hospitals

If your medical needs cannot be met at your doctor's office, you may need to go to the hospital. Hospitals have much more medical equipment for diagnosing and treating illnesses. They have rooms for doing surgery and for emergency medicine. They have rooms for patients to stay overnight, if necessary. Hospitals have staff on duty around the clock every day of the year.

Surgery Centers

Your doctor may recommend that you go to a surgery center rather than a hospital. Surgery centers are facilities that offer outpatient surgical care. This means that the patients do not stay overnight. They go home the same day they have the surgery. Serious surgeries cannot be done in a surgery center. They would be done in a hospital where the patient can stay and recover. For general outpatient care, many people go to clinics.

Clinics

Clinics are similar to doctors' offices and often have primary care physicians and specialists on staff. If you go to a clinic, you might not see the same doctor each time you go. You might see whoever is on duty that day. This might make it more difficult for the doctor to get to know you and your health issues. However, for people who do not need to go to the doctor often, a clinic might be a good fit.

Hospice Care

Hospice care provides a place where terminally ill patients can live out the remainder of their lives. Terminally ill patients will not recover from their illness. Hospice workers are specially trained and are experts in pain management. They are also trained and skilled at giving emotional support to the family and the patient. Many terminally ill patients receive hospice care in their own homes. Nurses visit the patient in their own home and provide medications for pain. They also spend time with family members, helping them learn to cope during the emotionally difficult time.

Pixtal/AGE Fotostock

Assisted Living Communities

As people get older, they may not be able to take care of themselves as well as they used to. Assisted living communities offer older people an alternative to nursing homes. In nursing homes, all of the resident's needs are taken care of. In assisted living communities, the residents can choose which services they need. They may be unable to drive and need transportation. They may need reminders to take medications. They may need to have food prepared for them. In an assisted living community, the residents are able to live in their own apartments as long as they are able. Medical staff is available when the residents need help.

PAYING FOR HEALTH CARE

Health care costs can be expensive. Many people buy health insurance to help pay for medical costs. Health insurance is a plan in which a person pays a set fee to an insurance company in return for the company's agreement to pay some or all medical expenses when needed. They pay a monthly premium, or fee, to the health insurance company for the policy. There are several different options when choosing health insurance.

Private Health Care Plans

One health insurance option is managed care. Health insurance plans emphasize preventative medicine and work to control the cost and maintain the quality of health care. Using managed care, patients save money when they visit doctors who participate in the managed care plan. There are several different managed care plans such as a health maintenance organization (HMO), a preferred provider organization (PPO), and a point-of-service (POS) plan.

Government Public Health Care Plans

The government currently offers two types of health insurance—Medicaid and Medicare. Medicaid is for people with limited income. Medicare is for people over the age of 65 and for people of any age with certain disabilities.

Following a logical plan can help you achieve many goals.

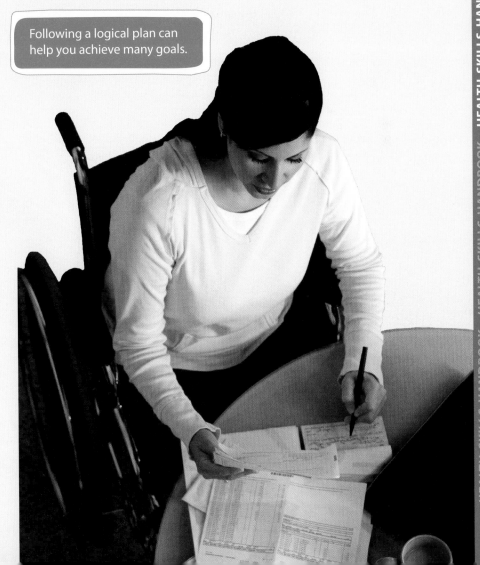

Building Healthy Relationships

LESSONS

MarkIT

 **PREMIUM ONLINE RESOURCES** >

 Audio

 Videos

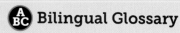 Bilingual Glossary

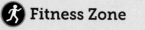 Fitness Zone

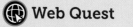 Web Quest

 Review

HAVE A GREAT DAY AT SCHOOL!!!

- Mom's Party SAT.9/3 @ 6PM
- "BIG GAME" THIS WEEKEND
- Need: Juice, Apples + Bread

AT PRACTICE
BE HOME
AROUND 7PM!

Many teens enjoy spending time together. *What activities do you enjoy with friends?*

Practicing Communication Skills

BIG IDEA ▷ Healthy relationships depend on good communication.

>>> **Before You Read**

QUICK WRITE List Make a list of all the people with whom you've communicated today. Have all your communications been with words?

▶ Video

>>> **As You Read**

FOLDABLES Study Organizer

Make the Foldable® on page 42 to record the information presented in Lesson 1.

>>> **Vocabulary**

› communication
› body language
› mixed message
› "I" messages
› active listening
› assertive
› aggressive
› passive

🔊 Audio

🔤 Bilingual Glossary

WHAT IS COMMUNICATION?

MAIN IDEA ▷ Communication involves your words, postures, gestures, and facial expressions.

You communicate with different people every day. Communication is *the exchange of information through the use of words or actions.* Communication involves sending and receiving messages, but it is more than just talking face-to-face. You communicate on the phone, in writing, and with your actions.

Communication is *more than* just **talking** face-to-face.

You use the phone to communicate with people you may not see every day. You communicate in writing with your teachers and online. E-mails and text messages let you share quick information, such as dates or directions. When you communicate by phone, in writing, and online, you use only your words. When you communicate in person, you also use your facial expressions and body language.

Verbal *and* Nonverbal Communication

When you talk to someone in person, you use your words. This is verbal communication. When you talk in person, others can see you, so your body language is also part of your communication. Body language is *postures, gestures, and facial expressions.* Your posture is how you hold your body. Gestures are motions you make with your hands. Body language is nonverbal communication—messages you send with your expressions and gestures.

When you talk to another person, do you look right at the other person? Do you show you care about the conversation? Your facial expressions show that you are truly interested in talking with the other person. Take the time to watch people as they talk. What does their body tell you about them as they talk?

>>> **Reading Check**

DEFINE *What is body language?*

©Creatas/PunchStock

Mixed Messages

If your words and your body language do not match, you may send mixed messages. A *mixed message* is *a situation in which your words say one thing but your body language says another.* If you feel shy or nervous, you might talk very quietly, or you might fidget with your hands.

You might not look directly at the person you are speaking to. An angry person might talk with his or her arms folded. If you are feeling embarrassed, you might look down instead of at the person you are talking to.

If your body language does not match the tone of your voice, you may send a mixed message.

For example, saying "I'm fine" in an angry tone might make others think something is wrong. A good communicator will look directly at someone and speak in a caring voice. Sometimes it can be difficult to understand a person who says one thing but who displays body language that sends a different message.

GOOD COMMUNICATION SKILLS

MAIN IDEA Good communication includes listening and showing that you understand what the other person is saying.

Good communication requires sending and receiving information that is understood by everyone involved. You send messages and receive messages by speaking, listening, and writing. It takes skills to be a good communicator. You need to be a good speaker, listener and writer to send and receive messages.

It takes *skills* to be a **good communicator**.

Speaking and listening in person is the most direct way to communicate. In person, the other person hears your words, and also sees your face and body. Your facial expressions and body language can tell a lot. If you look directly at the other person, you show attention and respect. If you smile, it looks as if you care.

If you look around or past the other person as you speak, you may look like you don't care about the conversation. If you look bored, you look like you don't care. If you hold your arms folded and stiff, you may appear too firm or disrespectful.

Body language is part of communication. *What message does this teen send with body language?*

> **» Reading Check**
> **DESCRIBE** *Name three examples of body language.*

Speaking and Listening Skills

Outbound ("Sending")	Inbound ("Receiving")
■ **Think, then speak.** Avoid saying the first thing that comes to mind. Plan what you're going to say. Think it through.	■ **Listen actively.** Recognize the difference between hearing and listening. Hearing is just being aware of sound. Listening is paying attention to it. Use your mind as well as your ears.
■ **Use "I" messages.** Express your concerns in terms of yourself. You'll be less likely to make others angry or feel defensive.	■ **Ask questions.** This is another way to show you are listening. It also helps clear up anything you don't understand. It prevents misunderstandings, which are a roadblock to successful communication.
■ **Make clear, simple statements.** Be specific and accurate. Stick to the subject. Give the other person a chance to do the same.	■ **Mirror thoughts and feelings.** Pay attention to what is being said. Repeat what someone says to show that you understand.
■ **Be honest with thoughts and feelings.** Say what you really think and feel, but be polite. Respect the feelings of your listener.	■ **Use appropriate body language.** Even if you disagree, listen to what the other person has to say. Make eye contact, and don't turn away.
■ **Use appropriate body language.** Make eye contact. Show that you are involved as a speaker. Avoid mixed messages. Beware of gestures, especially when speaking with people of different cultural backgrounds. Some gestures, such as pointing, are considered rude in certain cultures.	■ **Wait your turn.** Avoid interrupting. Let the person finish speaking. You'll expect the same courtesy when it's your turn.

Different skills are involved in sending and receiving messages. *Explain how these skills are related to one another.*

Speaking Skills

If you want to get your message across, you will need to develop good speaking skills. You can practice these guidelines to help you become a better speaker:

- **Think before speaking.** When you speak without thinking, you risk being misunderstood. Think about what you will say. You do not want to start talking without thinking about your words first.
- **Make clear, simple statements.** Be specific when you speak. Stay focused on the topic and on your message. Use examples when necessary to make your point more clear.

If you want to **get your** *message* **across,** you need **good** *speaking* **skills.**

- **Use "I" messages.** *"I" messages speak from your point of view to send a message.* For example, rather than saying, "You're not making sense," instead try saying, "I'm not sure what you mean."
- **Be honest.** Tell the truth to describe your thoughts and feelings. Be polite and kind.
- **Use appropriate body language.** Make eye contact. Think about your expressions and gestures. Show that you are paying attention.

Listening Skills

Listening skills are as important as speaking skills. Be an active listener. Active listening means *hearing, thinking about, and responding to another person's message.* You can develop these skills to become a good listener:

- **Pay attention.** Listen to what the speaker is saying. Think about that person's message as you are listening.
- **Use body language.** Face the speaker. Look at the speaker. Focus on the words you hear. Use your posture, gestures, and facial expressions to show that you are listening.
- **Wait your turn.** Before you ask questions or respond to what someone is saying, let that person finish speaking. Avoid interrupting someone.

- **Ask questions.** If it is appropriate, ask questions. Use "I" messages when you speak.
- **Mirror thoughts and feelings.** After the other person finishes speaking, repeat back in your own words what you believe that person said. This will show that you are listening. It will also help you better understand the message.

Writing Skills

When you write an e-mail, a text, or a note, remember that the person you are writing to cannot see you or hear your tone of voice. This may lead to misunderstandings. You can also practice basic skills for written communication:

- **Write clear, simple statements.** Be sure to state your thoughts and feelings clearly.
- **Reread your words before you send a message.** Again, the other person cannot see you. Make sure your thoughts can be clearly understood.

Make sure your written words say what you mean. *How can you be sure your message is clear?*

Russell Glenister/Corbis

Communicating *with* Parents *or* Guardians

Tyler has been dreaming of playing football for a while now. Tryouts for the local team are in two weeks. Tyler needs to talk to his parents first, but he is worried they will not understand how he feels about playing the sport. They want him to have enough time to do homework and study, and practices will take up a lot of time. Tyler is unsure about how to talk to his parents about playing football.

* State clear reasons for your request.

* Use "I" messages.

* Use a respectful tone and stay calm.

* Use appropriate listening skills.

* Be willing to compromise.

HAVE A GREAT DAY AT SCHOOL!!!

- Mom's Party SAT. 9/3 @ 6PM
- "BIG GAME" THIS WEEKEND
- Need: Juice, Apples + Bread

AT PRACTICE BE HOME AROUND 7PM!

With A Group

Write a script showing how Tyler talks to his parents about playing football. Use the techniques above to effectively communicate ideas, thoughts, needs, and feelings. Role-play your conversation for the class.

YOUR COMMUNICATION STYLE

MAIN IDEA Communication styles include assertive, aggressive, and passive.

Once you know *how* to communicate clearly, you can choose your communication *style*. A communicator can be *assertive*, *aggressive*, or *passive*. Each of these three communication styles has its own traits which can make communication either more or less effective.

A communicator can be **assertive**, **aggressive**, or **passive**.

An assertive communicator is friendly but firm. An asser-tive communicator *states his or her position in a firm but positive way.* For example, you tell a friend, "I need to be home on time because I promised my parents." An assertive communicator shows respect for himself or herself and others.

An aggressive communicator is someone who tends to be *overly forceful, pushy, hostile, or otherwise attacking in approach.*

Aggressive communicators may think too much about themselves and not show respect to others. For example, you tell a friend, "You'd better get me home on time." An aggressive communicator can hurt feelings or make others angry.

A passive communicator *has a tendency to give up, give in, or back down without standing up for his or her rights and needs.* For example, a passive communicator who has a firm curfew might tell a friend, "It doesn't matter when I get home." A passive communicator may care too much about what others think of him or her. Sometimes a passive communicator may not feel confidence or self-respect. You can change from being a passive communicator to an assertive communicator by reminding yourself that your thoughts and opinions have value.

>>> **Reading Check**

IDENTIFY *Which communication style is the most effective? Why?* ■

Cultural Perspectives

Differences in Body Language Body language is used in different ways in different cultures. For example, in many cultures of Southeast Asia, it is not considered appropriate to show facial expressions of sadness or anger. People from these cultures might smile to mask negative feelings or a negative statement. In other cultures, it is considered impolite to make eye contact when communicating with a member of the other gender. Certain hand and arm gestures often have different meanings in different cultures.

REVIEW

>>> **After You Read**

1. **DEFINE** What does *communication* mean?
2. **EXPLAIN** What is a mixed message?
3. **EXPLAIN** Which of the three communication styles do you think is most effective? Explain your answer.

>>> **Thinking Critically**

4. **HYPOTHESIZE** Imagine you have a friend who wants to copy your homework. Use "I" messages to respond.
5. **SYNTHESIZE** What are some nonverbal ways to show consideration for others?

>>> **Applying Health Skills**

6. **ANALYZING INFLUENCES** Pay attention to various conversations you see in school or on TV. Watch for an example of mixed messages in conversation. Describe the example.

🄲 Review

🔊 Audio

Family Relationships

BIG IDEA Your relationships with family members are some of the most important in your life.

Before You Read

QUICK WRITE Name the people you can talk to if you have a problem.

▶ Video

As You Read

STUDY ORGANIZER Make the study organizer on page 42 to record the information presented in Lesson 2.

Vocabulary

› family
› nurture
› role
› abuse
› physical abuse
› sexual abuse
› neglect

🔊 Audio

🔤 Bilingual Glossary

WHAT MAKES A FAMILY?

MAIN IDEA Family members support one another.

The way you relate with your family prepares you for how you relate to others for the rest of your life. A **family** is *the basic unit of society and includes two or more people joined by blood, marriage, adoption, or a desire to support each other.* Families come in many shapes, sizes, and types:

- A **couple** is two people who do not have children.
- A **nuclear family** is two parents and one or more children.
- An **extended family** is a nuclear family plus other relatives.
- A **blended family** has two adults and one or more children from a previous marriage.
- A **foster family** has adults caring for one or more children born to different parents.
- An **adoptive family** is a couple plus adopted children.
- A **joint-custody family** has two parents living apart and sharing custody of children.
- A **single-custody family** has parents living apart and children living with one parent.

Families Meet Needs

The main role of a family is to meet the needs of its members. Families provide food, clothing and shelter. They should also provide support and comfort. Healthy families nurture each member of the family. To **nurture** means *to fulfill physical needs, mental/emotional needs, and social needs.* A healthy family helps to nurture all sides of its members' health triangles:

- **Physical** Families care for their members by providing food, clothing and shelter.
- **Mental/Emotional** Family members offer love, acceptance, and support. They also pass along traditions, values, and beliefs. Your greatest influences in these areas often come from your family.
- **Social** Families teach their members how to get along with each other and with people outside the family..

> **▶▶ Reading Check**
>
> **DEFINE** *What is a family?*

Roles *and* Responsibilities *in the* Family

Every family member has a special role in the family. A **role** is *a part you play when you interact with another person.* Each role has certain responsibilities. Parents and other adults in a family have the responsibility of meeting the basic needs of the family. Parents also teach and model healthful behaviors and good communication skills.

Your role as a family member is to follow rules at home and to accept certain responsibilities.

If you have younger brothers or sisters, you may be a role model. Your role includes showing respect, caring, and appreciation. You can show that you respect your family by accepting your responsibilities. You can show appreciation by saying "thank you" to family members. You can also show caring by giving your time and attention to members of your family.

Family roles can change. As you get older, you will take on more responsibilities. You may be asked to help with younger or older members of your family.

You may take on more responsibilities in the home. Each time you accept a new responsibility, you show respect, love, and support for your family.

> *Every* family **member** has a *special role* in the family.

>>> **Reading Check**

RECALL *What are a parent's main family responsibilities?*

BUILDING STRONG FAMILIES

MAIN IDEA A strong family is built on good relationships.

People with strong family relationships feel connected. They feel safe and secure. This list offers guidelines for making and keeping strong family relationships:

- **Support one another.** Does your family believe in you? Knowing that you have support adds meaning when you succeed. Support can also help when you face a challenge.
- **Show appreciation for one another.** Families grow stronger when each member shows appreciation to the other members. For example, a child may say "Thank you for dinner," to parents or guardians. Another way to show appreciation for your family members is to help with tasks such as doing the dishes or folding the laundry.
- **Follow family rules.** Some rules are related to responsibilities, such as when to do your homework or when to take out the trash. Others rules can include what time to be home or when the TV can be on. Following the rules at home helps build trust and respect in a family.
- **Spend quality time together.** Take time for activities that include the whole family. Some families always have dinner together so they can talk about events of the day. Others plan evenings at home or weekend outings together.

Family responsibilities can change. *How is this teen showing a willingness to take responsibility as part of a family?*

- **Use good communication skills.** Talking openly helps solve problems and disagreements. Communication helps to develop trust and respect.
- **Show responsibility.** Do your tasks and chores without being asked. When you accept your family responsibilities, you show and model respect.
- **Show respect.** Speak to family members in a respectful tone of voice. Show respect for differences in family members.

Show respect for privacy and personal belongings.

>>> **Reading Check**

RECALL *Name three ways to build strong family relationships.*

CHANGES IN THE FAMILY

MAIN IDEA 〉 Families deal with change.

Changes and challenges affect every family. Change may occur with the birth of a baby, separation, divorce, or remarriage. You may take on new responsibilities, go to college, or start a job. Change may also occur with the loss of a job, illness or injury, military service, or moving to a new home. Strong relationships make it easier to cope with changes.

Communicating *openly* to family members can **help** *reduce stress*.

Sometimes family changes can cause you to worry or feel stress or sadness. When a family experiences change, it becomes more important for family members to communicate with one another.

Communicating openly with family members can help reduce stress. Talk about ways your role in the family might change. Sometimes outside help is needed to deal with serious change in the family structure. Family members may seek help from experts such as counselors, health care workers, religious leaders, legal experts, or law enforcement personnel.

Changes that happen in a family affect all family members. *What are some serious changes that can affect families?*

CHANGE	POSITIVE WAYS TO COPE
Moving to a new home	Before the move, look at a map of your new neighborhood. Find your new house, your school, and nearby parks. When in a new neighborhood, try to meet other teens.
Separation, divorce, or remarriage of parents	Tell both parents you love them. Talk to them or to another trusted adult about how you feel. A separation or divorce is not your fault.
Job change or job loss	If the family needs to limit spending for a while, ask how you can help.
Birth or adoption of a new sibling	Spend time with your new sibling. Ask your parents how you can help. Imagine what your relationship might be like in the future.
Illness or injury	Show that you care about a sick or injured family member by spending time with him or her and asking how you can help.
Death, loss, and grief	Accept the ways family members express grief. Don't expect their ways of coping to be the same as yours. Pay extra attention to younger members of the family.

Juan Silva/Stockbyte/Getty Images

SERIOUS FAMILY PROBLEMS

MAIN IDEA Serious family problems may require help from counselors or others.

Family problems can sometimes be serious and require outside help. Drug or alcohol addiction is a serious problem. While it may be that only one family member is addicted to drugs or alcohol, the whole family suffers. A family needs outside help to deal with drug or alcohol addiction.

A *parent* or *guardian* is **responsible** for caring for a *child's* **physical, mental/ emotional** and **social needs**.

A serious family situation that may require the help of police or other authorities is abuse. Abuse is *a pattern of mistreatment of another person.* Abuse can affect children or adults. Physical abuse involves *the use of physical force, such as hitting or pushing.* A person who is physically abused may shows bruises, scratches, burns, or broken bones. Emotional abuse can also be serious. Emotional abuse occurs when someone always yells or puts down another person. Emotional abuse can damage a person's self-esteem.

Sexual abuse is *any mistreatment of a child or adult involving sexual activity.* Sexual abuse is unwanted use of forced sexual activity including touching private body parts or being forced to touch body parts. Sexual abuse also includes showing sexual materials to a child. Abuse often includes secrets, and threats to keep secrets.

A parent or guardian is responsible for caring for a child's physical, mental/emotional and social needs. When a parent fails to provide proper care, he or she may be charged with neglect. Neglect is *failure to provide for the basic physical and emotional needs of a dependent.* Physical neglect can include not providing food, shelter, clothing, or medical care. Emotional neglect involves failing to give love and respect.

All forms of abuse and neglect are against the law. These kinds of serious family problems may also require outside help. Any person who feels abused or neglected must find someone who can help. The process of getting help can start by talking to another trusted adult, a teacher, a school counselor, or a medical professional.

> ## >> Reading Check
>
> **DEFINE** *What is abuse and what forms can it take?* ■

>> After You Read

1. **VOCABULARY** Define the word *neglect*.
2. **IDENTIFY** What are three ways to build and keep strong family relationships?
3. **EXPLAIN** Identify some family problems that would require outside help.

>> Thinking Critically

4. **SYNTHESIZE** Give some examples of ways you can use good communication skills with your family.
5. **COMPARE AND CONTRAST** Explain the difference between nurture and neglect.

>> Applying Health Skills

6. **ADVOCACY** Imagine you have a friend who you think may have a problem at home. Your friend is behaving in an unusual way. He or she seems sad, quiet and withdrawn. How can you communicate your concern to your friend?

Ⓒ Review

🔊 Audio

Peer Relationships

BIG IDEA Strong relationships will have a positive effect on your physical, mental/emotional, and social health.

Before You Read

QUICK WRITE List the people you consider your friends.

 Video

As You Read

STUDY ORGANIZER Make the study organizer on page 42 to record the information presented in Lesson 3.

Vocabulary

> peers
> acquaintance
> friendship
> reliable
> loyal
> sympathetic
> peer pressure
> assertive response

 Audio

Bilingual Glossary

WHO ARE YOUR PEERS?

MAIN IDEA Your peer group is made up of people who are close in age and have things in common with you.

As a teen, you spend a lot of time among your peers. Your **peers** are *people close to you in age who are a lot like you.* The students at your school and other teens you know from your outside activities are your peers. Peers will be an important part of your life throughout your lifetime. Think about all the peers you encounter in your daily life. Your peers may be your friends, classmates, teammates, or neighbors.

> ## *Peers* will be an **important** part of your *life* throughout your **lifetime**.

Your peers also include your acquaintances. An **acquaintance** is *someone you see occasionally or know casually.* Sometimes your acquaintances become friends. A peer can be someone you have never met but with whom you have something in common.

For example, if you volunteer for an agency that works for a clean environment, you are peers with other teens who volunteer for that agency. They may live in other cities or other countries, but they are still your peers.

Friendships During *the* Teen Years

During your teen years, you develop friendships with some of your peers and acquaintances. A **friendship** is *a relationship with someone you know, trust, and regard with affection.* Friendships usually begin with a common interest, such as a sport, a class in school, or conversations on the bus to or from school.

Your peers and acquaintances are the people around you. Your friends are the relationships you choose. Your friends may have a shared interest or the same values as you do. Having friends is an important part of your social health and growth. In strong friendships, you appreciate the values of loyalty, honesty, trust, and mutual respect.

What Makes a Good Friend?

Friendships share positive qualities and usually grow stronger with time. The traits of strong friendships apply equally to you and your friends. Strong, healthy friendships have a number of qualities in common:

- **Shared Values** Friendships can begin with shared values. If you are an honest, responsible person, you will appreciate honesty and responsibility in your friends. For example, if you work hard at school and are eager to learn, you share interests with other good students. If you take some responsibility for any of your younger siblings at home, your friends are likely to also have strong family relationships.
- **Reliability** A good friend is reliable. Reliable means *trustworthy and dependable.* Reliable friends do what they say they will do. They do not talk negatively to other people about their friends.

- **Loyalty** A good friend is loyal, or *faithful,* to his or her friends. In friendships that are strong, friends are loyal to each other. They agree to stick together not just in good times but also through any disagreements they may have. Good friends will respect and honor each other's personal interests, values, beliefs, and differences.

Friendships grow **stronger** with **time**.

- **Sympathy** Good friends share sympathy for one another. A sympathetic friend is *aware of how you may be feeling at a given moment.* For example, if you studied hard for a test but you did not do as well as you had hoped, you may feel sad or disappointed. A good friend will understand how you feel. The other person will listen if you want to talk about it and offer support.

- **Caring** A good friend cares about you. A friend can show caring by being interested in your feelings, your values, and your beliefs. A caring friend is a good listener and pays attention to you and your interests.
- **Trust** Good friends trust each other. They learn through their friendship that trust is important. Trust is proven through reliability and loyalty.
- **Respect** A good friend has self-respect. A good friend also has respect for his or her family, school, and friends. Good friends show respect by giving their time and attention to each other. You can show respect by displaying all the traits of friendship: reliability, loyalty, sympathy, caring and trust. Good friends also show their respect for each other's values and differences.

>> **Reading Check**

RECALL *Name three qualities of a good friend.*

Your peers are close to you in age and have a lot in common with you. *Describe some of the things this group of teens has in common with one another.*

Making New Friends

Teens typically find most of their friends at school, in their neighborhood, or in shared activities. Sometimes it can be hard to find new friends, such as when you change grades, schools, or move to a new neighborhood. However, you can develop skills to help make new friends.

- **Be yourself.** Identify your values, beliefs, and special interests. What would make you a good friend? You want to make friends who value you for who you are.
- **Break the ice.** Start a conversation with a compliment or a question. Show your interest. If the other person shares the same interest, you may be able to begin a new friendship.
- **Seek out teens who share your interests.** Join a club, sports team, or community group. There you will find peers who share some of the same interests you do.
- **Join a group that works for a cause you support.** You can show your citizenship and giving qualities to people who share your values. You will also help your community.

Sometimes it can be **hard to find** *new friends.*

Strengthening Friendships

Once you make a new friend, you will want to strengthen that friendship and help make it long-lasting. You can use a number of key strategies that can not only help you make new friendships but also help you make existing friendship stronger.

- **Spend time together.** The more time you spend with someone, the better you get to know each other. Do your homework together, share a special interest, practice a sport, or work on a school or community project together.
- **Communicate openly and honestly.** Open and honest communication will build trust and respect—qualities you want in your friendships.

An important part of keeping friendships strong is identifying problems and working to solve them. *These teens appear to be having a disagreement. What are they doing to resolve their dispute in a positive way?*

- **Help each other through hard times.** Good friendships aren't only about the fun times. Good friends also share their time and sympathy when a friend has a problem and may need support.
- **Respect each other's differences.** No two people are exactly alike. Show respect for the ways your friends may be different from you.
- **Encourage each other to reach goals.** An important part of friendship is sharing the interests and goals of others. Be giving of your time and attention, and be supportive of your friend's goals.
- **Identify problems and work to solve them.** A part of communication includes discussing problems and expressing your interest in solving a problem. It could be a problem your friend shares with you or a problem between you and a friend.

In order to communicate your interest in a friend, remember to think before speaking. Also practice being a good listener. Be honest and truthful about your feelings and opinions.

Talking about a problem with a friend can help both you and the other person understand your differences. It can also help you both better understand the issue and help find a solution to whatever problem the two of you may have.

PEER PRESSURE

MAIN IDEA ⟩ Peer pressure can affect you in different ways.

Teens spend much of their time among peers at school and in other activities. Peers influence some of the decisions that you make. *The influence that your peer group has on you* is **peer pressure.** Teens want to fit in and be accepted. Sometimes, without even knowing it, they are influenced by their peers. For example, if you notice that almost everyone at school wears zippered sweatshirts, you may want a zippered sweatshirt too.

You are influenced by what you see your peers do. This is called indirect peer pressure. No one is making you get a zippered sweatshirt, but you want one because you see everyone around you wears one.

You **always** have a **choice** to say no.

At other times, you may feel direct peer pressure. A peer might tell you what you should do to fit in or be accepted.

If you choose not to do what that person suggests, you may worry whether you will fit in and be part of the group. Remember that while your peers have a big influence on your life, you always have a choice to say no if you believe that a behavior or action will be harmful.

⟩⟩ Reading Check
DEFINE *Explain what indirect peer pressure is and give an example.*

Positive Peer Pressure

Like all influences, peer pressure can have a positive or negative effect. Positive peer pressure helps you make healthful choices. For example, if someone says "You are such a good dancer, we wish you would join the dance team," that is a positive suggestion. Dance may strengthen your physical health. You may also make new friends who have a shared interest.

Imagine that many of your peers volunteer at a food bank. They enjoy the sense of citizenship and caring. You may choose to volunteer too, based on your peers' positive experiences. Volunteering may make you feel good about yourself because you are helping others. You may make new friends. You are using an example you see in others to make a positive choice for yourself. This is positive peer pressure, or positive influence.

Positive examples set by others can have a major influence on your choices and decisions. *What are some other ways in which peer pressure can have a positive influence on you?*

McGraw-Hill Companies, Inc. Ken Karp, photographer

Negative Peer Pressure

Negative peer pressure may make decisions difficult. Your peers may urge you to do something you do not agree with or do not want to do. When you face negative peer pressure, you have a choice to make. It helps to think about your values. If you feel you have to choose between making a healthful choice or fitting in with a group, think about the consequences. True friends will respect your decision.

Encouraging a person to act in a way that is harmful or illegal is one form of negative peer pressure. Other forms may include dares, threats, teasing, or name-calling. You can recognize negative peer pressure by using the **H.E.L.P.** guidelines. **H.E.L.P.** stands for **H**ealthful, **E**thical, **L**egal, and **P**arent-approved. Would your choice affect your well-being or that of others? Would it show respect? Would your choice break the law? Would your parents approve?

If what your friends tell you to do does not meet the **H.E.L.P.** guidelines, you can refuse. All of your actions are your own choices, but you can learn ways to resist negative peer pressure.

- **Avoid the situation.** If you can tell that a situation might be unsafe, harmful, or against rules, do not participate.
- **Use assertive responses.** If your peers suggest a dangerous behavior or situation, say no. Use an assertive response, which *states your position strongly and confidently.*
- **Focus on the issue.** State your reasons for your choice. Avoid responding if your peers tease you. Avoid trading insults.
- **Walk away.** It is best to try to talk things out with peers who try to pressure you. If anyone gets angry, though, walk away.

>> **Reading Check**

EXPLAIN *Tell why negative peer pressure can be harmful or hurtful.* ■

Resisting peer pressure is a skill you can learn. *What are some effective ways you have found to handle negative peer pressure?*

REVIEW

>>> **After You Read**

1. **VOCABULARY** Define *friendship.*
2. **IDENTIFY** What are three ways to strengthen friendships?
3. **EXPLAIN** Define negative peer pressure and give an example.

>>> **Thinking Critically**

4. **COMPARE AND CONTRAST** Explain the consequences that both positive and negative influences from peers can have on a teen's life.
5. **SYNTHESIZE** What does H.E.L.P. stand for and why is it important?

>>> **Applying Health Skills**

6. **ANALYZING INFLUENCES** Do you think adults experience as much peer pressure as teens? Write a brief paragraph explaining your opinion.

Ⓒ Review

◀⑴ Audio

Hands-On HEALTH ACTIVITY

WHAT YOU WILL NEED

* Pencil or pen
* Paper

WHAT YOU WILL DO

1 Working in pairs, imagine a situation in which "you" messages might occur. Think of your own "you" message. Write the situation on the top of the paper. Write the "you" message below on the left. Change that into an "I" message, writing the "I" version on the right.

2 Here are three sample situations:
• Your older brother was late picking you up. He had no excuse.
• A classmate told a lie about you.
• Your sister borrowed something and returned it in poor condition.

3 Read each "you" message to the rest of the class. Then read the corresponding "I" message.

WRAPPING IT UP

Was the "you" message or "I" message most effective? Explain why. Think of a disagreement you have had with a family member or friend. How could using "I" messages have helped resolve the conflict? How does practicing positive behaviors, such as using "I" messages when you communicate, benefit your overall health?

"I" Messages

Communicating effectively is especially important when there is a disagreement.

When you use "I" messages, you express your feelings. "I" messages are unlike "you" messages, which place blame on the other person. To help see the difference, compare these two statements:

• **"You" message:** You always get your way! You're selfish!

• **"I" message:** Sometimes I would like to have a say in what we do.

This activity will allow you to practice sending "I" messages. If you practice this skill, you will become a better communicator.

READING REVIEW

FOLDABLES and Other Study Aids

Take out the Foldable® that you created for Lesson 1 and any study organizers that you created for Lessons 2–3. Find a partner and quiz each other using these study aids.

LESSON 1 Practicing Communication Skills

BIG IDEA Healthy relationships depend on good communication.

* Communication is the exchange of information through the use of words or actions.
* Communication involves your words, postures, gestures, and facial expressions.
* Body language is postures, gestures, and facial expressions.
* A mixed message is a situation in which your words say one thing but your body language says another.
* Good communication includes listening and showing that you understand what the other person is saying.
* "I" messages speak from your point of view to send a message.
* Active listening means hearing, thinking about, and responding to another person's message.
* Communications styles include assertive, aggressive, and passive.

LESSON 2 Family Relationships

BIG IDEA Your relationships with family members are some of the most important in your life.

* A family is the basic unit of society and includes two or more people joined by blood, marriage, adoption, or a desire to support each other.
* Family members support one another.
* To nurture means to fulfill physical needs, mental/emotional needs, and social needs.
* A strong family is built on good relationships.
* Families learn to deal with change.
* Serious family problems, such as abuse, addiction, or neglect, may require help from counselors or others.
* Neglect is the failure of parents to provide their children with basic physical and emotional care and protection.

LESSON 3 Peer Relationships

BIG IDEA Strong relationships will have a positive effect on your physical, mental/emotional, and social health.

* Your peer group is made up of people who are close in age and have things in common with you.
* Qualities of friendship include shared values, reliability, loyalty, sympathy, caring, trust, and respect.
* Peer pressure can affect you in positive or negative ways.
* Using H.E.L.P. guidelines can help you make healthful choices when you face negative peer pressure.

Review

Web Quest

ASSESSMENT

Reviewing Vocabulary *and* Main Ideas

> family
> body language

> verbal
  communication

> nurture
> role

> neglect

>> On a sheet of paper, write the numbers 1–6. After each number, write the term from the list that best completes each statement.

LESSON 1 **Practicing Communication Skills**

1. Expressing your feelings, thoughts, and experiences in words, through speaking or writing, is _____.

2. _____ includes posture, gestures, and facial expressions that send messages.

3. The part you play when you interact with another person is known as a _____.

LESSON 2 **Family Relationships**

4. The _____ is the basic unit of society and includes two or more people brought together by blood, marriage, adoption, or a desire for mutual support.

5. To _____ is to fulfill physical, mental/emotional, and social needs.

6. _____ is failure to provide for the basic physical and emotional needs of a dependent.

>> On a sheet of paper, write the numbers 7–12. Write *True* or *False* for each statement below. If the statement is false, change the underlined word or phrase to make it true.

LESSON 3 **Peer Relationships**

7. The influence that people your own age have on you is called <u>nurturing</u>.

8. You can use the <u>H.E.L.P.</u> criteria to resist negative peer pressure.

9. <u>Trust</u> is a trait of good friendships.

10. Friends urging you to come to a party where there might be alcohol is an example of <u>positive</u> peer pressure.

11. An <u>acquaintance</u> is someone you see occasionally or know casually.

12. An <u>aggressive response</u> states your position strongly and confidently.

✔ eAssessment

>> Using complete sentences, answer the following questions on a sheet of paper.

🌥️ *Thinking* **Critically**

13. **ANALYZE** How do positive relationships affect your physical and mental/emotional health? Explain your answer.

14. **ASSESS** What are some qualities you look for in a friend? How would those qualities affect your mental/emotional and social health?

15. **INFER** How can learning how to resist negative peer pressure improve all sides of your health triangle?

🎷 *Write* **About It**

16. **DESCRIPTIVE WRITING** Design a greeting card for someone who has had a positive influence on your life. Write a message for the inside of the card that includes specific examples of how that person has positively influenced your life.

17. **NARRATIVE WRITING** Write a skit that shows a situation in which a teen uses each step of the H.E.L.P. guidelines to resist negative peer pressure and make a healthful choice.

Ⓐ Ⓑ Ⓒ Ⓓ STANDARDIZED TEST PRACTICE

Writing
Read the directions in the left column below and refer to the example in the right column.

Directions:
Write a letter to persuade your principal to organize more after-school activities. Begin your letter by stating your viewpoint. Then provide concrete examples of activities you think would be valuable to students. In addition, list benefits you feel these activities would have, and explain them in your letter. Use a respectful but firm tone to persuade the principal to see your point of view. Use the example in the next column to give you ideas about the way you should structure your letter.

Example:
Did you know that strong friendships and positive peer pressure add to a student's school success and overall good health? It's true! One of the best ways to forge strong friendships is through after-school activities. This is why I think our school should provide more after-school activities such as clubs and organizations. I think this is a good idea for several reasons: First, after-school activities would strengthen relationships between students. Second, students would have a safe place to go to after school. Third, teens would have fun and make new friends.

BUILDING HEALTHY RELATIONSHIPS

Have you ever considered all the time and energy you put into maintaining positive, healthy relationships with your friends, parents, siblings, teachers—even your girlfriend or boyfriend? Healthy relationships require attention.

FAMILY

Your family is the single greatest influence on developing your values.

TYPES OF FAMILIES

FAMILY TYPE	MAKEUP
Couple	Two people who do not have children
Nuclear	Two parents and one or more children
Extended	A nuclear family plus other relatives such as grandparents
Single-parent	One parent and one or more children
Blended	Two people, one or both with children from previous marriages
Foster	Adults caring for one or more children born to different parents
Adoptive	A couple plus one or more adopted children
Joint-custody	Two parents living apart, sharing custody of their children
Single-custody	Two parents living apart and one or more children living with only one parent

WHAT MAKES A SOLID FAMILY?

SUPPORT · APPRECIATION · RESPECT · TOGETHERNESS · FOLLOWING FAMILY RULES

FRIENDS

Your friends are those in your peer group with whom you have the most in common and most enjoy spending time with. Friendships, unlike family relationships, are ones that you freely choose.

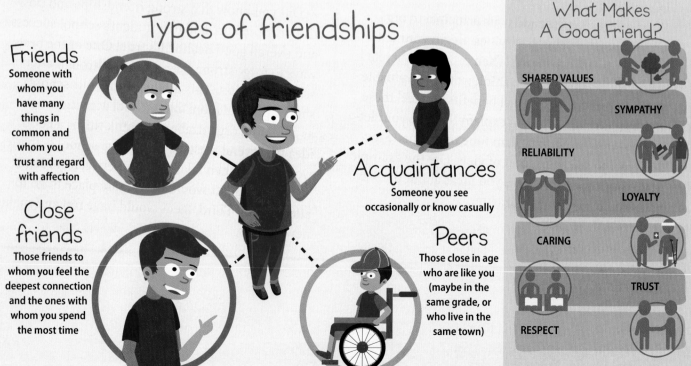

Types of friendships

Friends
Someone with whom you have many things in common and whom you trust and regard with affection

Close friends
Those friends to whom you feel the deepest connection and the ones with whom you spend the most time

Acquaintances
Someone you see occasionally or know casually

Peers
Those close in age who are like you (maybe in the same grade, or who live in the same town)

What Makes A Good Friend?

SHARED VALUES

SYMPATHY

RELIABILITY

LOYALTY

CARING

TRUST

RESPECT

FORMING CLOSER RELATIONSHIPS

During your teen years, you will become interested in forming closer friendships and new kinds of relationships.

ADOLESCENCE BRINGS CHANGE

Relationships become deeper and more important during the teen years.

Your friends may also begin to include more members of the opposite gender.

Consider your future

The places you go and the people you spend time with can have consequences that affect your safety, health, and plans for your future.

List the goals you want to achieve to get a better idea of what limits you need to set to help you reach your goals.

STARTING TO DATE
Group dating

Spending time with a group of your peers is a way to get to know others in a low-stress environment.

Going out with a group can help you discover new interests and learn more about activities you enjoy.

Healthy dating relationships

* Mutual respect
* Caring
* Honesty
* Loyalty
* Commitment

SAYING NO TO RISK BEHAVIORS

Using the S.T.O.P. strategy can help you deal with negative peer pressure. You can use one or all of the following steps:

SAY NO IN A FIRM VOICE. State your feelings firmly but politely. Make your "no" sound like you mean it. Use body language to support your words.

TELL WHY NOT. Explain why you feel the way you do. Do not apologize. Just say, "No, thanks. I care about my health."

OFFER OTHER IDEAS. Suggest an alternative activity that is safe and fun.

PROMPTLY LEAVE. If all else fails, let your actions match your words. Simply walk away from the situation.

Dating Relationships and Abstinence

PREMIUM ONLINE RESOURCES 〉

 Audio   Videos 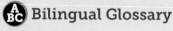 Bilingual Glossary

 Fitness Zone  Web Quest   Review

Friendships take on a greater importance during the teen years. *What qualities do you think make a good friend?*

Beginning *to* Date

BIG IDEA ▶ Your friendships become more important during adolescence.

Before You Read

QUICK WRITE Write a short paragraph that describes how your friendships with boys and girls have changed over the last few years.

▶ Video

As You Read

FOLDABLES Study Organizer

Make the Foldable® on page 43 to record the information presented in Lesson 1 about beginning to date.

Vocabulary

› commitment
› affection

🔊 Audio

🔤 Bilingual Glossary

Developing Good Character

Respect Every relationship benefits from respect. One way to show respect is through simple courtesies—for example, holding the door for the person behind you. Using good manners at someone else's home is another sign of respect. What ways can you think of to show respect for someone you are dating?

CHANGING FRIENDSHIPS

MAIN IDEA ▶ Changes during the teen years include making new friends and forming new types of friendships.

You have learned that a friendship is a relationship between two people that is based on trust, caring, and consideration. People often choose friends with similar interests and values. Good friends can benefit your health in many ways. They can have a positive influence and help you resist harmful behaviors.

The teen years are a time of growth. This time, or adolescence, brings physical, mental/emotional, and social changes. During puberty, your body starts to develop the physical traits of an adult. Your brain also changes, and you start to see the world in more complex ways.

You may begin to try to understand yourself and how you fit into society. Teens will also discover new interests, including making new friends. You may also start to develop different types of friendships.

Thinking *about* Dating

Relationships become more important during the teen years than they did when you were younger. As you grow and mature, your friendships may change. You still share good times and have fun with your friends and acquaintances, but you also begin seeking deeper qualities in the people you choose as friends. These qualities may include loyalty and trust. Your group of friends may also begin to include more members of the opposite gender.

How have your *friendships* **changed** as you have **grown?**

During the teen years, you may also develop feelings of attraction. For example, it may be that the girl across the street was just another neighbor. Now you might pay more attention to her when she is around.

Brand X Pictures/PunchStock

When you were younger, maybe your brother's best friend used to annoy you. Now you might find yourself worrying about how you look when he visits.

These kinds of new feelings cause some teens to begin to think about dating. Dating is a way to get to know people better. There is no specific time when you are supposed to start dating. Some people feel ready to date while in their teens. Others do not feel ready to start dating until much later.

Group Dating

Choosing to spend time with a group of your peers is one way to date and get to know others. For example, a mixed group of teens may get together to watch a movie or play a game. Other fun group activities might include hiking, dancing, skating, or playing sports. These kinds of activities also have the benefit of keeping you physically active. Some other advantages to going out as part of a group include:

- **Conversation** It is generally easier to keep conversation going when several teens are out together. Everyone can talk less and listen more.
- **Less Pressure** You will likely feel less pressure to engage in sexual activity and other risk behaviors when you go out as part of a group.
- **Less Expense** A group date can be less expensive for each individual because everyone in the group can help share the cost of an activity.

Group dating offers chances to grow and mature. You can learn how to communicate with different types of people. Going out with a group can help you learn more about activities you enjoy. It may help you discover new interests as you learn about other people. Group dating may even lead you to meet someone you would like to get know to better as an individual.

Spending time in a group activity is one alternative to individual dating. *Tell why you think these teens enjoy one another's company.*

Individual Dating

As you continue to grow and become more mature, you may want to go out on a date with just one person. Individual dating is a big step that should be taken for the right reasons. Peer pressure is not a good reason to begin individual dating. You should wait until you are ready to date. Your parents may also let you know when they feel you are ready for individual dating.

How will you know whether you would like to date someone? You may find that you enjoy being around one person in particular. You may also find that you share common interests and values. At some point, you may agree that you would like to spend time together by going on a date. You can think of dating as a special form of friendship. As is the case with any other friendship, a healthy dating relationship is based on caring, honesty, and respect.

Dating is a way to **get to know people** better.

Individual dating is not always stress-free. You may feel nervous going out for the first time. You may worry about what your date will think of you. These thoughts and feelings may be new to you, but many people think and feel the same way before a date. Dating as a teen involves developing a different type of friendship than those you had when you were younger. A date does not have to mean the start of a lifelong commitment, which is *a pledge or a promise.* Going on an individual date may turn out to be just the first step in making a special new friend.

>> **Reading Check**

EXPLAIN *Why is spending time in a group a good alternative to individual dating?*

Healthful Ways to Show Affection

Another change that happens during the teen years is the development of feelings of *affection,* or *feelings of love for another person.* Most people want to find someone special to care about deeply. It is one of the great gifts and joys of life. Showing affection can take many different forms. One form of showing affection is sexual intimacy. However, it is more healthful to postpone sexual activity until adulthood and marriage.

Show that you are a **good friend** by *listening* and **being sympathetic.**

However, teens can show affection in healthful ways. Holding hands and hugging are physical ways to show affection, but you can also do something thoughtful for another person. You might give a friend a card or a small gift as a way to show affection. For example, Bethany has a big soccer game coming up. Her friend Justin likes to create healthful meals and snacks, so he makes Bethany a tray of fruits and vegetables to share with her teammates. Bethany knows Justin has an important test later this week, so she sends him an encouraging note.

You can show that you are a good friend by listening and being sympathetic to the other person's thoughts and ideas. These kinds of actions deepen the bonds of affection. They also display good character, which is a sign that you are maturing. ■

Showing affection in a healthy way lets someone know that you care. *Explain why you think it is important to show someone that you care.*

>>> **After You Read**

1. **DEFINE** What does the term *relationships* mean?
2. **IDENTIFY** Name three advantages of dating in a group.
3. **LIST** Name two healthful ways for teens to show affection.

>>> **Thinking Critically**

4. **APPLY** If you were thinking of dating someone, what characteristics might you look for in the other person?
5. **EXPLAIN** Discuss some reasons that dating may not be right for everyone.

>>> **Applying Health Skills**

6. **EVALUATE** Adam and Emily have been dating for a while. Adam is expressing that he thinks they should engage in more physical affection. What would you advise Emily to tell him?

🔄 Review

🔊 Audio

Healthy Dating Relationships

BIG IDEA Engaging in unhealthful behaviors, such as sexual activity, carry consequences that can seriously affect your future.

>> **Before You Read**

QUICK WRITE Identify some risks involved in sexual activity. Write a couple of sentences explaining them.

▶ **Video**

>> **As You Read**

STUDY ORGANIZER Make the study organizer on page 43 to record the information presented in Lesson 2.

>> **Vocabulary**

> sympathetic
> consequences
> limits
> dating violence
> abstinence

🔊 **Audio**

🔤 **Bilingual Glossary**

Myth vs. Fact

Myth: People with good character and values never get STDs.

Fact: Anyone can get an STD. If you do not know your partner's history of sexual activity, you cannot know whether that person has an STD.

HEALTHY DATING RELATIONSHIPS

MAIN IDEA Healthy dating relationships involve healthful boundaries and healthful ways of showing affection.

Remember that a dating relationship is a special kind of friendship. Qualities of good friendships include reliability and loyalty. Good friends support you and keep their promises. Good friends are also trustworthy and **sympathetic,** or *aware of how you may be feeling at a given moment.* They allow you to share your thoughts and emotions. When you decide to date individually, it is important that you and your dating partner establish healthful boundaries. The qualities of healthful dating relationships have much in common with those of good friendships.

Thinking *about* Your Future

As you grow and mature, you will become more independent. Adults will not always be present to set limits for you and make sure that you stay within them. Setting your own limits will become very important. What you do can have serious **consequences,** or *the results of actions.*

The places you go and the people you spend time with can affect your safety, health, and plans for the future. You will need to evaluate situations and avoid negative influences. Remember to use refusal skills when you are pressured to do something you are not ready to do.

A *dating relationship* is a special kind of **friendship.**

One way to establish limits in your own life and avoid these consequences is to write down the goals you want to achieve. Once you understand what you want to achieve, you will have a better idea of what limits, or boundaries, you need to set to help you reach your goals.

>> **Reading Check**

EXPLAIN *What is one way to help establish limits in your own life? How would setting limits help you?*

Setting Limits

Imagine playing a game or sport that had no rules. The activity would seem confusing, and it could also be dangerous. Rules bring order and purpose to games, and they serve a similar purpose in daily life. Rules can take the form of limits, or *invisible boundaries that protect you.* Among the many common examples of limits are the laws that society sets and lives by.

You probably have limits that your parents or guardians set at home. Those limits might include what TV shows you can watch, what websites you can visit, and how late you can stay up at night. Like laws, these limits are intended to keep you safe and to protect you. Rules for using the Internet, for example, may keep you away from dangerous or inappropriate sites.

Good communication skills are one characteristic of healthy dating relationships. *Describe how these teens are demonstrating good communication skills.*

In addition, having a set bedtime helps to ensure that you will get the sleep you need as a growing teen. These are all examples of ways your parents may try to promote good health and prevent illness. However, while your parents set certain limits, you must also learn to identify healthful limits for yourself.

Respecting Yourself *and* Your Date

Healthy friendships tend to bring out the best in each person. Healthy dating relationships should do the same thing. Qualities of healthy friendships and healthy dating relationships include mutual respect, caring, honesty, and commitment.

You can also use communication, cooperation, and compromise to help build a healthy dating relationship. For example, you may want to go for a hike, while your date may want to play disc golf. A compromise might be a trip to a park that has a disc golf course. Sometimes compromise is not the best choice to resolve a disagreement.

You should not compromise if the result would be harmful or unlawful. You should also avoid compromising on things that really matter to you, such as your values and beliefs.

Healthy dating *relationships* should **bring out the best** in each *person*.

Practicing abstinence also reflects the respect you have for yourself and for others. Remember, if you want to show someone that you care for that person, you can do so in ways that do not involve sexual activity. You can practice being kind and considerate. You can also offer support by talking and listening to the other person.

>>> **Reading Check**

EXPLAIN *What is one way to help establish limits in your own life? How would setting limits help you?*

Respect Both you and your date deserve to be treated with consideration and respect.

Communication When you are with someone you are dating, you should be yourself and communicate your thoughts and feelings honestly.

No Pressure You should never feel pressured to do anything that goes against your values or your family's guidelines.

McGraw-Hill Companies, Inc. Ken Karp, photographer

Vicky Kasala/Getty Images

A sexual relationship can be emotionally demanding for most teens. *Explain the mental/emotional consequences that can result from sexual activity as a teen.*

Dating Violence

Healthy dating relationships are built on respect. Violence of any type is a sign of an unhealthy relationship and also shows a lack of respect. For example, *when a person in a dating relationship tries to control his or her partner,* he or she is committing <u>dating violence.</u> Dating violence can include physical, emotional, or psychological abuse.

Teens who are just starting to date are not always sure how to have a healthy dating relationship. If a dating relationship feels uncomfortable or becomes violent, it is important to tell a parent or other trusted adult right away. If your dating partner becomes violent or abusive, avoid the relationship.

When a Dating Relationship Ends

Most dating relationships formed during the teen years do not last. One or both dating partners may simply change or outgrow the relationship. Whatever the reason for a breakup, the loss of a special relationship can be difficult to cope with. Breaking up can result in stress and depression. When a dating relationship ends, it is natural and normal to feel lonely and hurt. However, these feelings fade with time.

If it is the other person who decides to break up, it can be even more painful. However, the healthiest thing you can do is to respect the other person's wishes. Accept that person's decision and find a way to move on. It may not be healthful to start another dating relationship right away. Eventually, though, you will find another person with similar interests, values, and goals who you would like to get to know better.

>>> **Reading Check**

IDENTIFY *What are two examples of limits for teens?*

CONSEQUENCES OF EARLY SEXUAL ACTIVITY

MAIN IDEA Choosing abstinence is a way to avoid the physical consequences of sexual activity.

As teens begin individual dating, they may face new pressures. Among these is the pressure to engage in sexual activity. The Internet, movies, TV, popular music, and magazines may suggest that sexual activity among young people is common. The media and other influences may make it look like normal behavior.

The choice to be *sexually abstinent* promotes good health.

In truth, most teens avoid sexual activity. The Centers for Disease Control and Prevention (CDC) conduct a Youth Risk Behavior Surveillance Survey (YRBSS) every two years. In 2011, the survey showed that just six percent of teens under the age of 13 have engaged in sexual activity.

You may read and hear about sexual activity among teens in magazines, music, and online. Maybe you feel pressure from your friends. However, you can choose not to engage in sexual activity. You can practice sexual abstinence, or *the conscious, active choice not to participate in high-risk behaviors.*

The choice to be sexually abstinent as a teen promotes good health. It helps teens avoid the risks that accompany sexual activity. Sexual abstinence shows that you are focusing on your current goals and your plans for the future. It also shows respect for the physical and emotional well-being of others. It is important to understand that being sexually active can have serious consequences. Sexual activity can affect all three sides of your health triangle—physical, mental/emotional, and social.

The choices you make have consequences that will affect your future. *Identify some healthful limits you can set for yourself to help you achieve your goals.*

Physical Consequences

Teens who become sexually active expose themselves to a number of risks. Becoming sexually active brings the risk of being infected with a sexually transmitted disease (STD). STDs can damage the reproductive system and prevent a person from ever having children. Some STDs remain in the body for life—even after they are diagnosed and treated. Other sexually transmitted diseases, especially HIV/AIDS, can result in death. Any type of sexual activity can result in an STD.

Another risk of early sexual activity is unplanned pregnancy. Most teens do not have the emotional maturity to become parents. Teens usually do not have the financial resources to take care of a baby. The teen years are a time for thinking about what you want to do with the rest of your life. Teens who become parents usually must put their own education and career plans on hold. When people wait until adulthood to become parents, they are better able to achieve their long-term goals.

⟩⟩ Reading Check

IDENTIFY *What are some specific physical consequences of early sexual activity?*

Chase Jarvis/Getty Images

Mental/Emotional Consequences

Teens who become sexually active may also experience other consequences. Some of these consequences may affect a teen's mental/emotional health. The consequences can include:

- **Emotional distress** because one or both partners are not committed to each other.

When a **dating relationship** ends, it is *natural* and *normal* to feel **lonely and hurt.**

- **Loss of self-respect** because sexual activity may go against their personal values and those of their families.
- **Guilt** over concealing their sexual activity from their parents and others.
- **Regret and anxiety** if sexual activity results in an unplanned pregnancy, an STD, or the breakup of the relationship with the partner.

Teen parenthood can be difficult both emotionally and financially. *List some other challenges that this teen might face.*

Social Consequences

Sexual activity can also affect a teen's social health. Becoming sexually active can limit a teen's interest in forming new friendships. The teen years are a time to meet new people and explore new interests. A teen who is involved in an exclusive relationship with one other person may not be open to meeting new people. In addition, an unplanned pregnancy can limit a teen's plans for the future. For teens who become parents, caring for a baby and raising a child must become their first priority.

> **》》Reading Check**
> EXPLAIN *Why might teens experience regret and anxiety from a sexual relationship?* ■

PhotoDisc/Getty Images

》》After You Read

1. **DEFINE** What does *consequences* mean? Use the term in an original sentence.
2. **LIST** Name the types of consequences that can result from engaging in sexual activity.
3. **IDENTIFY** What are three possible mental/emotional consequences of teens engaging in sexual activity?

》》Thinking Critically

4. **ANALYZE** What are some qualities that good friendships and healthy dating relationships have in common?
5. **EXPLAIN** What are three benefits of abstaining from sexual activity?

》》Applying Health Skills

6. **EVALUATE** How can sexually transmitted diseases (STDs) affect a teen both now and in the future?

🔄 Review

🔊 Audio

Abstinence *and* Saying No

BIG IDEA ⟩ Practicing refusal skills will help you deal with peer pressure.

Before You Read

QUICK WRITE List three ways of saying no when someone pressures you to do something dangerous or unhealthy.

▶ **Video**

As You Read

STUDY ORGANIZER Make the study organizer on page 43 to record the information presented in Lesson 3.

Vocabulary

› risk behaviors
› refusal skills

🔊 **Audio**

🔤 **Bilingual Glossary**

🏃 Fitness Zone

Physical Fitness Plan One way a friend can give positive peer pressure is by promoting healthful activities such as exercise. You might set up a regular time to play sports or go for a run or hike with your friends. Sharing a fitness routine can help build stronger relationships and improve everyone's physical and emotional well-being.

CHOOSING ABSTINENCE

MAIN IDEA ⟩ Choosing abstinence involves communication with your dating partner, self-control, avoiding risky situations, and using refusal skills.

One of the most important limits you can set for yourself is choosing abstinence from risk behaviors, or *actions that might cause injury or harm to you or others.* This includes avoiding sexual activity. When you begin dating, choosing abstinence is the healthful choice. Many teens are making this choice. The CDC's Youth Risk Behavior Survey shows that percentage of teens choosing abstinence is steadily increasing.

> One of the most **important limits** you can set is *choosing abstinence.*

Committing *to* Abstinence

Abstinence is a choice you will have to recommit to each time you face pressure to engage in sexual activity. Even if you have been sexually active in the past, you can still choose abstinence.

It is important to talk about your decision with the person you date. These tips may help the conversation go more smoothly:

- Choose a relaxed and comfortable time and place.
- Begin on a positive note, perhaps by talking about your affection for the other person.
- Be clear about your reasons for choosing abstinence.
- Be firm in setting limits in your physical relationship.

To stay firm in your decision, continue to remind yourself of your limits and the reasons you are choosing abstinence in the first place.

Dealing *with* Sexual Feelings

Practicing abstinence requires planning and self-control. Sexual feelings are normal and healthy. You cannot prevent them, but you do have control over how you deal with them. Teens can learn ways to manage these feelings. The tips on the next page can help you to maintain self-control and practice abstinence.

©Radius Images/Corbis

- **Set limits on expressing affection.** Think about your priorities and set limits for your behavior before you are in a situation where sexual feelings may develop.
- **Communicate with your partner.** Make sure your dating partner understands and respects your limits.
- **Talk with a trusted adult.** Consider asking a parent or other trusted adult for suggestions on ways to manage your feelings and emotions.
- **Avoid risky situations.** Choose safe, low-pressure activities, such as a group date.
- **Date someone who respects and shares your values.** A dating partner who respects you and has similar values will understand your commitment to abstinence.

>> **Reading Check**

ANALYZE *Why is it important to discuss your commitment to abstinence with your dating partner?*

Avoiding Risky Situations

Where you go and what you do can have a big impact on your health and safety. Here are some basic precautions:

- **Before you go on a date, know where you are going and what you will be doing.** Find out who else will be there, and discuss with your parents or guardians what time they expect you home.
- **Avoid places where alcohol and other drugs are present.** These substances can impair a person's judgment. People under the influence of alcohol or other drugs are more likely to take part in risk behaviors, including sexual activity.
- **Avoid being alone on a date.** You may find it more difficult to maintain self-control when you and your date are alone together. One-on-one situations also increase the risk of being forced or pressured into sexual activity. Group dating can be a healthful alternative.

Saying No to Risk Behaviors

It's Saturday night, and Zoe is at a party at a friend's house. It seems like fun at first, but Zoe soon realizes that her friend's parents are not home and that some of the people at the party are older. Zoe notices a lot of people smoking and drinking alcohol. Some couples are finding places in the house to be alone. Zoe decides that this party is not for her and calls her parents to pick her up. While she's waiting, someone offers her a cigarette and a beer and asks her to go upstairs.

With A Group

Write a paragraph explaining how Zoe could use the S.T.O.P strategy to refuse the cigarette and beer and the offer to go off alone with someone else. The strategy below is detailed on the next page:

- Say no in a firm voice.
- Tell why not.
- Offer another idea.
- Promptly leave.

Communication and respect are signs of a good relationship. *Explain how setting limits with your dating partner can help strengthen your relationship.*

SW Productions/Getty Images

USING REFUSAL SKILLS

MAIN IDEA › You can use and practice refusal skills to help you keep your commitment to abstinence.

Think about some of the reasons you decided to commit to abstinence. You will need to remember them if you are ever pressured. Abstinence is not a decision you can make once and never think about again. You can use refusal skills, or *strategies that help you say no effectively,* to help maintain your decision.

Peer pressure can be **negative** or **positive.**

Taking basic precautions to avoid high-risk situations can help you enjoy dating in your teens. *Explain why it is important to know where you are going and what you will be doing on a date.*

Refusal skills take practice. The S.T.O.P. strategy can be an effective way to say no to risk behaviors. The letters in S.T.O.P. represent the four steps of the strategy. You can use one or all of the following steps:

- **Say no in a firm voice.** State your feelings firmly but politely. Say, "No, I don't want to." Make your no sound like you really mean it. Use body language to support your words. Make eye contact with the person.
- **Tell why not.** If the other person keeps up the pressure, explain why you feel the way you do. You do not need to use phony excuses or make up reasons. Just say, "No, thanks, I care about my health." Do not apologize. You have done nothing wrong.

- **Offer other ideas.** If the person pressuring you to do something is a friend, you might suggest alternatives. Instead of something that has risks, suggest an activity that is safe and fun instead.
- **Promptly leave.** Sometimes, firmly saying no, explaining why not, and suggesting alternatives may not work. If all else fails, just walk away and leave the situation. Let your actions match your words. If you need a ride home, phone a parent or other trusted adult to come and pick you up.

›› **Reading Check**

IDENTIFY *What is a refusal strategy you might use when being pressured to do something you do not want to do?*

Know where you are going, what you will be doing, and when you will be home.

Avoid places where alcohol and other drugs are present.

Avoid being alone on a date at home or in an isolated place.

DEALING WITH PRESSURE

MAIN IDEA Knowing how to respond to people who want you to do something you do not want to do will help you resist that pressure.

Most of your friends are probably your peers—the people close to you in age who have a lot in common with you. Sometimes teens worry about what their friends think. Your friends' opinions can affect how you act. The influence your peer group has on you is called peer pressure. Peer pressure can be negative or positive.

Negative Peer Pressure

Friends should not pressure you to do something that is unsafe or unhealthful. They should not pressure you to do something that goes against your values or your family's values. True friends will respect your choices.

By using refusal skills, you stand up for your values and build self-respect. You also show others you have strength and character. *Identify the S.T.O.P. strategy step this teen appears to be taking.*

Encouraging a person to act in a way that is harmful or illegal is one form of negative peer pressure. It can also come in the form of dares, threats, teasing, name-calling, or bullying. Use refusal skills and have responses ready for those who try to get you to do something negative.

Positive Peer Pressure

Positive peer pressure is when true friends suggest that you do the right thing. They may encourage you to study more, work on a project together, or welcome new people into the group. Friends can also help you say no to risk behaviors. Positive peer pressure can be good for you. It can improve your health and safety and also help you feel better about yourself.

>>> Reading Check

DEFINE *What is* peer pressure? ■

LESSON 3

REVIEW

>>> After You Read

1. **DEFINE** Explain what the term *risk behavior* means. Use it in an original sentence.
2. **LIST** List four ways to help keep a commitment to abstinence.
3. **IDENTIFY** Give one example of positive peer pressure and one of negative peer pressure.

>>> Thinking Critically

4. **EVALUATE** Jay has told Ron twice that he does not want to sneak into the school basketball game. Jay has even offered to pay for Ron's ticket, but Ron insists on sneaking in. What should Jay do next?

>>> Applying Health Skills

5. **APPLY** Write a skit about a situation in which a teen uses each step of the S.T.O.P. strategy to refuse to participate in a risk behavior.

↻ Review

♬ Audio

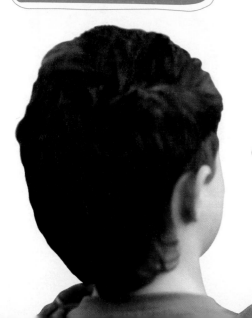

Hands-On HEALTH ACTIVITY

A Taste *of* Parenthood

Many teens do not understand how demanding parenthood can be. This brief experiment will give you a glimpse of the responsibilities.

WHAT YOU WILL NEED

* Help of a parent, guardian, or sibling
* Clock or watch with an alarm feature
* Paper and pencil or pen

WHAT YOU WILL DO

1 Select a time when you have a light workload. Arrange with a family member to help you.

2 Go about your normal activities, such as watching TV or speaking to a friend on the phone.

3 Without warning, your partner is to set off the alarm. Stop what you are doing and turn off the alarm. The interruption represents the attention a baby requires.

4 Note the time you heard the alarm and what you were doing when it went off.

5 Return to your normal activities. Your partner is to set the alarm off a minimum of five times.

WRAPPING IT UP

Write about your experiment. What would it be like to respond to such an alarm every day? How might it be similar to caring for a child? Share your report with classmates and compare your experiences.

READING REVIEW

FOLDABLES and Other Study Aids

Take out the Foldable® that you created for Lesson 1 and any study organizers that you created for Lessons 2–3. Find a partner and quiz each other using these study aids.

LESSON 1 Beginning to Date

BIG IDEA Your friendships become more important during adolescence.

* Changes during the teen years include making new friends and forming new types of friendships.
* Dating is a way to get to know other people better.
* Some people start dating while in their teens, but others do not feel ready to date until much later.

LESSON 2 Healthy Dating Relationships

BIG IDEA Healthy dating relationships involve healthful boundaries and healthful ways of showing affection.

* Qualities of healthy relationships include mutual respect, caring, honesty, and commitment.
* Growing up involves establishing limits in order to avoid risks and consequences so that you can achieve your goals in life.
* Choosing abstinence is a way to avoid the physical consequences of sexual activity.

LESSON 3 Abstinence and Saying No

BIG IDEA Practicing refusal skills will help you deal with peer pressure.

* Choosing abstinence involves communication with your dating partner, self-control, avoiding risky situations, and using refusal skills.
* Abstinence is a choice you will have to recommit to each time you face pressure to engage in sexual activity..
* It is normal and healthy to have sexual feelings, but you can control them instead of letting sexual feelings control you.
* You can use and practice refusal skills to help you keep your commitment to abstinence.
* Knowing how to respond to people who want you to do something you do not want to do will help you resist that pressure.
* The S.T.O.P strategy (Say no in a firm voice; Tell why not; Offer other ideas; Promptly leave) can be an effective way to say no to risk behaviors.

 Review

 Web Quest

ASSESSMENT

Reviewing Vocabulary *and* Main Ideas

› abstinence   › affection   › consequences
› sympathetic   › commitment   › limits

» On a sheet of paper, write the numbers 1–6. After each number, write the term from the list that best completes each statement.

LESSON 1 **Beginning to Date**

1. A _____ is a pledge or a promise to someone.

2. Feelings of love for another person are also known as _____.

LESSON 2 **Healthy Dating Relationships**

3. Good friends are _____, meaning they understand how you may be feeling at a given moment.

4. The invisible boundaries that protect you, or _____, include the laws that society uses.

5. The places you go and the people you spend time with can have _____ that affect your personal safety, health, and plans for your future.

6. _____ is the conscious, active choice not to participate in high-risk behaviors.

» On a sheet of paper, write the numbers 7–12. Write True or False for each statement below. If the statement is false, change the underlined word or phrase to make it true.

LESSON 3 **Abstinence and Saying No**

7. <u>Consequences</u> are actions that might cause injury or harm to you or others.

8. Teens should practice <u>abstinence</u> when it comes to risk behaviors.

9. Encouraging a person to act in a way that is harmful or illegal is one form of <u>sympathy.</u>

10. Part of developing good refusal skills is learning how to apply the <u>S.T.O.P. formula.</u>

11. A teen who practices abstinence from risk behaviors <u>will</u> experience negative legal consequences.

12. Abstinence from <u>risk behaviors</u> includes avoiding tobacco, alcohol, drug use, and sexual activity.

 eAssessment

>> Using complete sentences, answer the following questions on a sheet of paper.

☁ *Thinking* **Critically**

13. ANALYZE Della was invited to a get-together at the home of a friend's friend. When she arrived, Della found out that the girl's parents were not home and saw others drinking and smoking. What would be an assertive way for Della to let her friend know she is not interested in staying at the party?

14. INFER What effect does abstaining from risk behaviors have on your relationships?

➤ *Write* **About It**

15. NARRATIVE WRITING Write a skit that shows a situation in which a teen uses each step of the S.T.O.P. formula to refuse to participate in a risk behavior.

16. DESCRIPTIVE WRITING Write a blog post describing ways in which choosing abstinence from risk behaviors can benefit all sides of your health triangle.

Ⓐ Ⓑ Ⓒ Ⓓ STANDARDIZED TEST PRACTICE

Writing

Read the prompts below. On a separate sheet of paper, write an essay that addresses each prompt. Use information from the chapter to support your writing.

1. Imagine that a friend is considering engaging in a sexual activity. Write a dialogue in which you describe setting personal limits and the benefits of remaining abstinent before marriage.

2. Write an essay discussing why it is important to use assertive refusal skills rather than passive responses when dealing with peer pressure.

CHAPTER 1

Foldables®

Make this Foldable® to help organize what you learn in Lesson 1 about practicing communication skills.

1 Begin with a plain sheet of notebook paper. Fold the sheet of paper in half along the long axis.

2 Turn the paper, and fold it into thirds.

3 Unfold and cut the top layer along both fold lines. This makes three tabs. Draw two overlapping ovals.

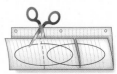

4 Label the left tab *Verbal,* the middle tab *Communication,* and the right tab *Nonverbal.*

Write the definitions and examples of verbal and nonverbal communication under the appropriate tab. Under the middle tab, describe how both types of communication help to share feelings, thoughts, and information.

Study Organizers

Use the following study organizers to record the information presented in Lessons 2–3.

Lesson 2:
K-W-L Chart

K	W	L

Lesson 3:
Key Word Cluster

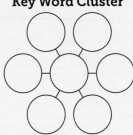

CHAPTER 2

Foldables®

Make this Foldable® to help organize what you learn in Lesson 1 about beginning to date.

1 Begin with a plain sheet of notebook paper. Draw a straight line across the middle of the page to divide it in half.

2 Fold the top and bottom quarters of the page to meet the line in the middle.

3 Next, fold the page in half.

4 Cut along the creases you have made in the top and bottom flaps.

5 On the four flaps you have created, write *Thinking about Dating, Group Dating, Individual Dating,* and *Healthy Ways to Show Affection.*

List the main ideas from this lesson under each of the appropriate tabs.

Study Organizers

Use the following study organizers to record the information presented in Lessons 2–3.

**Lesson 2:
K-W-L Chart**

K	W	L

**Lesson 3:
Four Section Chart**

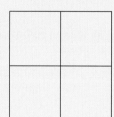

Glossary/Glosario

English

Abstinence (AB stuh nuhns) The conscious, active choice not to participate in high-risk behaviors.

Abuse (uh BYOOS) The physical, emotional, or mental mistreatment of another person.

Acquaintance Someone you see occasionally or know casually.

Active listening Hearing, thinking about, and responding to another person's message.

Advocacy Taking action in support of a cause.

Affection Feelings of love for another person.

Aggressive Overly forceful, pushy, hostile, or otherwise attacking in approach.

Assertive Willing to stand up for yourself in a firm but positive way.

Assertive response A response that declares your position strongly and confidently.

Attitude (AT ih tood) Feelings and beliefs.

Body language Postures, gestures, and facial expressions.

Commitment A pledge or a promise.

Communication The exchange of information through the use of words or actions.

Conflict resolution A life skill that involves solving a disagreement in a way that satisfies both sides.

Consequences The results of actions.

Cultural background The beliefs, customs, and traditions of a specific group of people.

Culture the collected beliefs, customs, and behaviors of a group

Cumulative (KYOO myuh luh tiv) risk When one risk factor adds to another to increase danger.

Español

abstinencia Opción activa y conciente de no participar en comportamientos de alto riesgo.

abuso Maltrato físico, emocional o mental de otra persona.

conocido Alguien a quien ves ocasionalmente o conoces casualmente.

audición activa Oír el mensaje de otra persona, pensar en el mensaje y responder.

promoción Actuar en apoyo de una causa.

afecto Sentimiento de amor hacia otra persona.

agresivo(a) Excesivamente forzoso, hostil o de otra manera, que ataca durante el acercamiento.

firme Dispuesto a defenderse de manera resuelta y positiva.

reacción agresiva Reacción que establece tu posición con fuerza y confianza.

actitud Sentimientos y creencias.

lenguaje corporal Posturas, gestos, y expresiones faciales.

compromiso Promesa o voto.

comunicación Intercambio de información a través del uso de palabras y acciones.

resolución de un conflicto Habilidad que implica el hecho de resolver un desacuerdo satisfaciendo a los dos lados.

consecuencias Resultados de los actos.

base cultural Creencias, costumbres y tradiciones de un grupo específico de personas.

cultura Colección de creencias, costumbres y comportamientos de un grupo.

riesgo acumulativo Cuando un factor riesgoso se suma a otro e incrementa el peligro.

English

Español

D

Dating violence When a person uses violence in a dating relationship to control his or her partner.

relacion violenta Cuando una persona usa violencia en una relación amorosa para poder controlar a su pareja.

Decision making The process of making a choice or solving a problem.

tomar decisiones Proceso de hacer una selección o de resolver un problema.

E

Environment (en VY ruhn muhnt) All the living and nonliving things around you.

medio Todas las cosas vivas y no vivas que te rodean.

F

Family The basic unit of society and includes two or more people joined by blood, marriage, adoption, or a desire to support each other.

familia Unidad básica de la sociedad que incluye dos o mas personas unidas por sangre, matrimonio, adopción o el deseo de ser soporte el uno del otro.

Friendship A relationship with someone you know, trust, and regard with affection.

amistad Relación con una persona que conoces, en la que confías, y aprecias con afecto.

G

Goal setting The process of working toward something you want to accomplish.

establecer metas Proceso de esforzarte para lograr algo que quieres.

H

Health The combination of physical, mental/emotional, and social well-being.

salud Combinación de bienestar físico, mental/emocional y social.

Health care system All the medical care available to a nation's people, the way they receive the care, and the way the care is paid for.

sistema de cuidado de la salud Servicios médicos disponibles para a la gente de una nación y las formas en las cuales estos son pagados.

Health insurance A plan in which a person pays a set fee to an insurance company in return for the company's agreement to pay some or all medical expenses when needed.

seguro médico Plan en el que una persona paga una cantidad fija a una compañía de seguros que acuerda cubrir parte o la totalidad de los gastos médicos.

Health skills skills that help you become and stay healthy

habilidades de salud Habilidades que ayudan a ser y mantenerte saludable.

Heredity (huh RED I tee) The passing of traits from parents to their biological children.

herencia Transferencia de características de los padres biológicos a sus hijos.

I

"I" message A statement that presents a situation from the speaker's personal viewpoint.

mensaje yo Declaración que presenta una situación desde el punto de vista personal del orador.

Glossary/Glosario

English

Lifestyle factors Behaviors and habits that help determine a person's level of health.

Limits Invisible boundaries that protect you.

Long-term goal A goal that you plan to reach over an extended period of time.

Loyal faithful

Managed care A health insurance plan that saves money by encouraging patients and providers to select lest costly forms of care.

Media Various methods for communicating information.

Mind-body connection How your emotions affect your physical and overall health and how your overall health affects your emotions.

Mixed message A situation in which your words say one thing but your body language says another.

Neglect Failure to provide for the basic physical and emotional needs of a dependent.

Nurture Fulfill physical, mental, emotional, and social needs.

Passive A tendency to give up, give in, or back down without standing up for rights and needs.

Peer pressure The influence that your peer group has on you.

Peers People close to you in age who are a lot like you.

Physical abuse the use of physical force

Prevention Taking steps to avoid something.

Preventive care Steps taken to keep disease or injury from happening or getting worse.

Primary care provider Health care professional who provides checkups and general care.

Español

factores del estilo de vida Conductas y hábitos que ayudan a determinar el nivel de salud de una persona.

límites Barreras invisibles que te protegen.

meta a largo plazo Objetivo que planeas alcanzar en un largo periodo de tiempo.

leal Fiel.

cuidado controlado Plan de seguro médico que ahorra dinero al limitar la selección de doctores de las personas.

medios de difusión Diversos métodos de comunicar información.

conexión de la mente con el cuerpo Forma en la cual tus emociones afectan tu salud física y general, y como tu salud general afecta tus emociones.

mensaje contradictorio Situación en que tus palabras expresan algo pero tu lenguaje corporal lo contradice.

abandono Fallas en el proceso de proveer las necesidades físicas y emocionales de una persona considerada como dependiente.

criar Satisfacer necesidades físicas, mentales, emocionales y sociales.

pasivo Tendencia a renuncia, dejar de lado, o hacerse atrás sin reclamar derechos o necesidades.

presión de pares Influencia que tu grupo de compañeros tiene sobre ti.

compañeros Personas de tu grupo de edad que se parecen a ti de muchas maneras.

abuso físico Uso de fuerza física.

prevención Tomar pasos para evitar algo.

cuidado preventivo Medidas que se toman para evitar que ocurran enfermedades o daños o que empeoren.

profesional médico principal Profesional de la salud que proporciona exámenes médicos y cuidado general.

English

Refusal skills Strategies that help you say no effectively.

Reliable Trustworthy and dependable.

Risk The chance that something harmful may happen to your health and wellness.

Risk behavior An action or behavior that might cause injury or harm to you or others.

Role A part you play when you interact with another person.

Sexual abuse Sexual contact that is forced upon another person.

Short-term goal A goal that you can achieve in a short length of time.

Specialist (SPEH shuh list) Health care professional trained to treat a special category of patients or specific health problems.

Stress The body's response to real or imagined dangers or other life events.

Sympathetic (simp uh THET ik) Aware of how you may be feeling at a given moment.

Values The beliefs that guide the way a person lives.

Wellness A state of well-being or balanced health over a long period of time.

Español

R

habilidades de rechazo Estrategias que ayudan a decir no efectivamente.

confiable Confiable y seguro.

riesgo Posibilidad de que algo dañino pueda ocurrir en tu salud y bienestar.

conducta arriesgada Acto o conducta que puede causarte daño o perjudicarte a ti o a otros.

papel Parte que tú desempeñas cuando actúas con otra persona.

S

abuso sexual Contacto sexual forzado por una persona.

meta a corto plazo Meta que uno puede alcanzar dentro de un breve periodo de tiempo.

especialista Profesional del cuidado de la salud que está capacitado para tratar una categoría especial de pacientes o un problema de salud específico.

estrés Reacción del cuerpo hacia peligros reales o imaginarios u otros eventos en la vida.

solidario Estar consciente que como te puedes estar sintiendo en un momento indicado.

V

valores Creencias que guían la forma en la cual vive una persona.

W

bienestar Mantener una salud balanceada por un largo período de tiempo.

Index

Index

Index

FLIP 4 FITNESS

Flip for Fitness is for everyone. Non-athletes who avoid joining organized sports can develop a personal fitness plan to stay in shape. Even athletes can use some of the tips to cross train for their favorite sport.

Planning a Routine

Flip for Fitness helps you plan a fitness routine that helps your body slowly adjust to activity. Over time, you will increase both the length of time you spend and the number of times that you are physically active each week. Teens should aim to get at least one hour of physical activity each day. These periods of physical activity can be divided into shorter segments, such as three 20 minute segments each day. Exercise includes any physical activity, such as completing a fitness plan, playing individual or group sports, or even helping clean at home. The key is to keep your body moving.

Before You Start Exercising

Every activity session should begin with a warm-up to prepare your body for exercise. Warm-ups raise your body temperature and get your muscles ready for physical activity. Easy warm-up activities include walking, marching, and jogging, as well as basic calisthenics or stretches. As you increase the time you spend doing a fitness activity, you should increase the time you spend warming up. Check the Sample Physical Fitness Plan in Teen Health in Connect Ed.

Fitness Information *and* Resources

Fitness Apps *and* Other Resources

»  **USDA's MyPlate** The MyPlate Super Tracker is a free online fitness and diet tracker. To review the tracker, go online to https://www.choosemyplate.gov and search for "Super Tracker".

» Additionally, organizations such as the **American Heart Association** and **KidsHealth** provide resources on developing walking programs. The online addresses are: http://startwalkingnow.org and http://kidshealth.org.

» Finally, smartphone and tablet users can download several nutrition and fitness tracking apps. Many are free of charge. Use the terms "fitness", "exercise", or "workout" when searching for apps.

Accessing Information

» The *Teen Health* online program includes resources to develop your own fitness plan. Check out the **Fitness Zone** resources in ConnectEd.

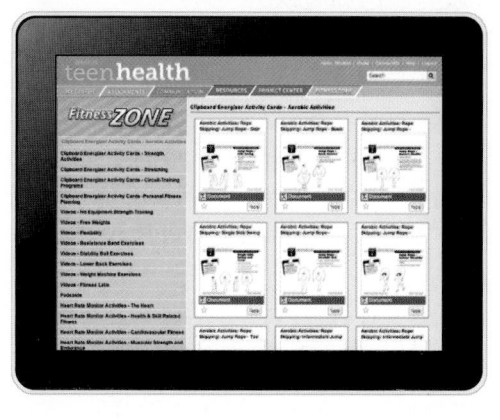

» The Centers for Disease Control and Prevention's, **Body & Mind (BAM)** web site also provide fitness information. The online address is: http://www.bam.gov. Search for "physical activity" or "activity cards."

Safety Tips

On the following pages, you'll find fitness activities for groups or individuals. Each activity includes information on what you'll need, how to start, and how to stay safe. Safety is the most important factor.

⚠ Always be aware of where you are and don't take any unnecessary chances.

⚠ Obey the rules of the road while riding your bicycle, avoid unsafe areas, and use the proper safety equipment when working out.

⚠ Finally, remember to drink water and to rest between exercise sessions.

5 Elements *of* Fitness

When developing a fitness plan, it's helpful to have a goal. Maybe your goal is to comfortably ride your bike to school each day or maybe you want to complete the Tour de France in the future. Regardless of the reasons why you develop a fitness plan, focusing on the five elements of fitness will help you achieve overall physical fitness. The five elements are:

1 Cardiovascular Endurance
The ability of the heart and lungs to function efficiently over time without getting tired. Familiar examples are jogging, walking, bike riding, and swimming.

2 Muscle Endurance
The ability of a muscle or a group of muscles to work non-stop without getting tired. Many activities that build cardiovascular endurance also build muscular endurance, such as jogging, walking, and bike riding.

3 Muscle Strength
The ability of the muscle to produce force during an activity. Activities that can help build muscle strength include push-ups, pull-ups, lifting weights, and running stairs.

4 Flexibility
The ability to move a body part freely, without pain. Improve your flexibility by stretching gently before and after exercise.

5 Body Composition
The amount of body fat a person has compared with the amount of lean mass, which is bone, muscle, and fluid. A healthy body is made up of more lean mass and less body fat. Body composition is a result of diet, exercise, and heredity.

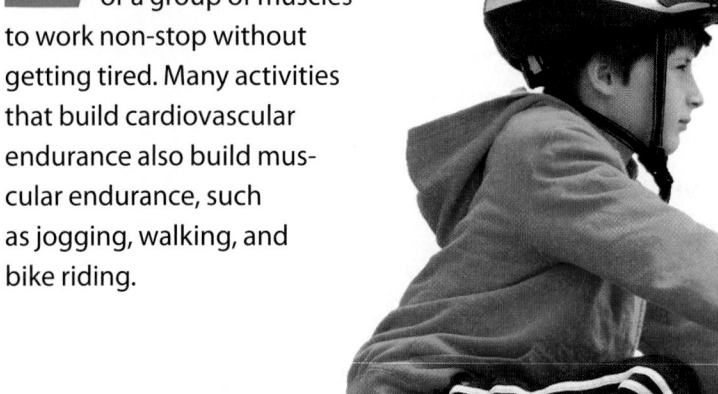

Fitness Circuit

Are you looking for a quick workout that will develop endurance, strength, and flexibility? A Fitness Circuit may be just what you need. Many public parks have Fitness Circuits (sometimes called Par Courses) with exercise stations located throughout a park. You walk or run between stations as part of your workout. A fitness circuit can also be created in your backyard or even a basement.

What Will I Need?

» Access to a public park or a home-made Fitness Circuit course.

» Comfortable workout clothes that wick away perspiration.

» Athletic shoes.

» Stopwatch (optional).

» Jump rope, dumbbells, exercise bands, or check out the Fitness Zone Clipboard Energizer Activity Cards, Circuit Training for ideas.

How Do I Start?

» In the park, read the instructions at each exercise station and perform the exercises as shown. Use the correct form. Try to do as many repetitions as you can for 30 seconds.

» After you finish the exercise, walk or run to the next station and complete that exercise.

» Check your heart rate to see how intensely you exercised at the end of the Fitness Circuit.

» Every month or so, consider adding a new exercise.

How Can I Stay Safe?

» Be alert to your surroundings in a public park. It is best to have a friend with you. It's also more fun to exercise with a friend.

» At home, leave enough room between stations to allow you to move and exercise freely. Avoid clutter in your exercise area.

» Perform the exercises correctly and at your own pace.

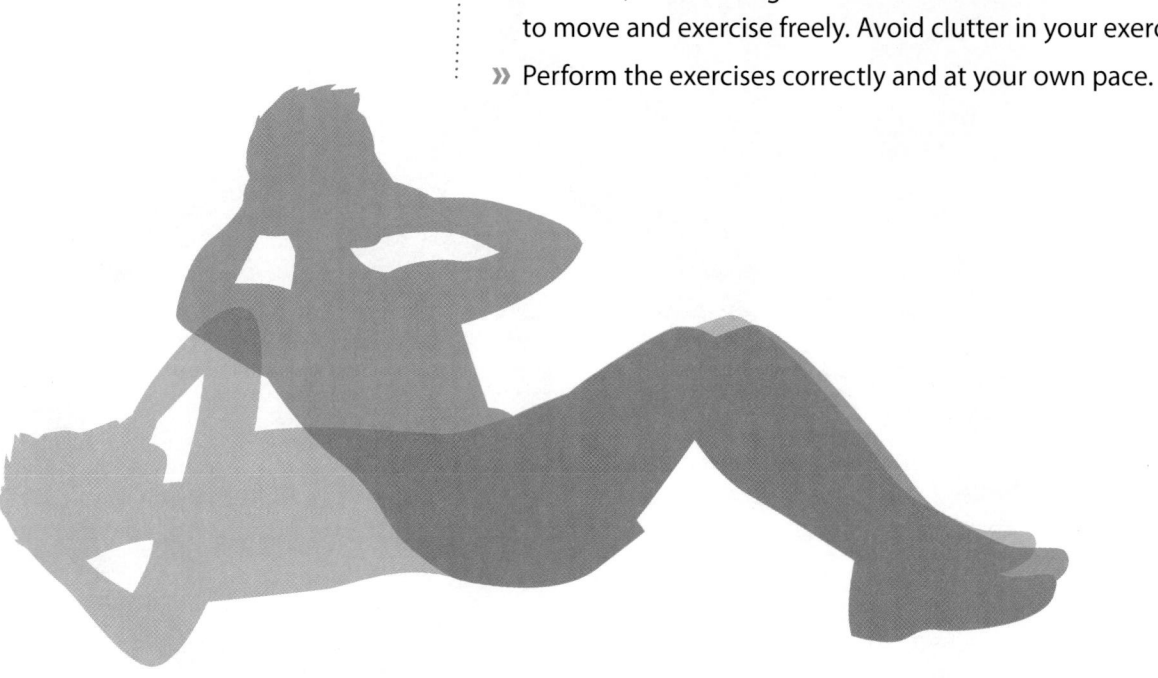

Walking

Walking is more than just a way to get from one place to another. It's also a great physical activity. By walking for as little as 30 minutes each day you can reduce your risk of heart disease, manage your weight, and even reduce stress. Walking requires very little equipment and you can do it almost anywhere. More good news: Walking is also something you can do by yourself or with friends and family.

What Will I Need?

» Running or walking shoes. Many athletic shoe stores sell both.

» Loose comfortable clothes that wick away perspiration. Layering is also a good idea. Consider adding a hat, sunglasses, and sunscreen if needed.

» Stopwatch and water bottle unless there are water fountains on your route.

» A pedometer or GPS to track your distance.

How Do I Start?

» Five minutes of easy stretching.

» Walk upright with good posture. Do not exaggerate your stride or swing your arms across your body.

» Build your time and distance slowly. One mile or 20 minutes every other day may be enough for the first couple weeks. Eventually you will want to walk at least 30-60 minutes five days a week.

How Can I Stay Safe?

» Let your parents know where you will be walking and how long you will be gone.

» Avoid wearing headphones if by yourself or if walking on a road or street.

Running *or* Jogging

Running or jogging is one of the best all-around fitness activities. Running uses the large muscles of the legs thereby burning lots of calories and also gives your heart and lungs a good workout in a shorter amount of time. Running also helps get you into condition to play team sports like basketball, football, or soccer. More good news is that running can be done on your schedule although it's also fun to run with a friend or two.

What Will I Need?

» A good pair of running shoes. Ask your Physical Education teacher or an employee at a specialist running shop to help you choose the right pair.

» Socks made of cotton or another type of material that wicks away perspiration.

» Bright colored or reflective clothing and shoes.

» A stopwatch or watch with a second sweep to time your runs or track your distance.

» Optional equipment might include a jacket or other layer depending on the weather, sunscreen, and sunglasses.

How Do I Start?

Your ultimate goal is to run at least 20 to 30 minutes at least 3 days a week. Use the training schedule shown below. Start by walking and gradually increasing the amount of time you run during each exercise session. Starting slowly will help your muscles and tendons adjust to the increased work load. Try spacing the three runs over an entire week so that you have one day in-between runs to recover.

How Can I Stay Safe?

» Use the correct equipment for the sport you have chosen.

» Running on a track, treadmill, or in a park with level ground will help you avoid foot or ankle injuries.

» Avoid running on the road, especially at night.

» Avoid wearing headphones unless you are on a track, treadmill, or another safe place. Safety experts agree that headphones can distract you from being alert to your surroundings.

Here is a plan to get you started as a runner:

» Start each run with a brisk 3-5 minute walk to warm-up.

» Take some time to slowly stretch the muscles and areas of the body involved in running. Avoid "bouncing" when stretching or trying to force a muscle or tendon to stretch when you start to feel tightness.

» Begin slowly and gradually increase your distance and speed. A good plan for the first several weeks is to alternate walking with easy running. The running plan included in this section can give you some tips on how to train for a 5K run.

» Use the "talk test." Can you talk in complete sentences during your training runs? If not, you are running too fast.

Training Schedule

M W F	Split Schedule	Duration
Week 1	Brisk 5 min. walk Walk: 60 - 90 seconds Run: 60 seconds	Repeat for 20 min.
Week 2 and 3	Brisk 5 min. walk Walk: 60 seconds Run: 60 - 90 seconds	Repeat for 20 min.
Week 4	Brisk 5 min. walk Walk: 60 seconds Run: 3 - 5 minutes	Repeat for 20 min.
Week 5+	Brisk 5 min. walk Run: 20 to 30 minutes	

Preparing *for* Sports *and* Other Activities

Do you want to play a sport? If so, think about developing a fitness plan for that sport. Some of the questions to ask yourself are: Does the sport require anaerobic activity, like running and jumping hurdles? Does the sport require aerobic fitness, like cross-country running? Other sports, such as football and track require muscular strength. Sports like basketball require special skills like dribbling, passing, and shot making. A workout plan for that sport will help you get into shape before organized practice and competition begins.

What Will I Need?

Each sport has different equipment requirements. Talk to a coach or physical education teacher about how to get ready for your sport. You can also conduct online research to learn what type of equipment you will need, such as:

» Proper footwear and workout clothes for a specific sport.

» What facilities are available for training and practice, such as a running track, tennis court, football or soccer field, or other safe open area.

» Where you can access weights and others form of resistance training as part of your training.

How Do I Start?

Now that your research is done, you can create your fitness plan. Include the type of exercises you will do each training day.

» Include a warm-up in your plan.

» List the duration of time that you will work out.

» Plan to exercise 3–5 days a week doing at least one kind of exercise each day. Remember to include stretching before every workout.

How Can I Stay Safe?

» Get instruction on how to use free weights and machines

» Make sure you start every activity with a warm-up.

» Ease into your fitness plan gradually so you do not pull a muscle or do too much too soon.

» Practice good nutrition and drink plenty of water to stay hydrated.

Interval Training

Getting fit takes time. One method, interval training, can show improvement in two weeks or less. Interval training consists of a mix of activities. First you do a few minutes of intense exercise. Next, you do easier, less-intense activity that enables your body to recover. Interval training can improve your cardiovascular endurance. It also helps develop speed and quickness.

Intervals are typically done as part of a running program. Not everyone wants to be a runner though. Intervals can also be done riding a bicycle or while swimming. On a bicycle, alternate fast pedaling with easier riding. In a pool, swim two fast laps followed by slower, easier laps.

What Will I Need?

» A running track or other flat area with marked distances like a football or soccer field.

» If at a park, 5–8 cones or flags to mark off distances of 30 to 100 yards.

» A training partner to help you push yourself (optional).

How Do I Start?

» After warming up, alternate brisk walking (or easy jogging). On a football field or track, walk 30 yards, jog 30 yards, and then run at a fast pace for 30 yards. Rest for one minute and repeat this circuit several times. If at a park, use cones or flags to mark off similar distances.

» Accelerate gradually into the faster strides so you stay loose and feel in control of the pace.

» If possible, alternate running up stadium steps instead of fast running on a track. This will help your coordination as well as your speed. Running uphill in a park would have similar benefits.

How Can I Stay Safe?

» Interval training works the heart and lungs. For this reason, a workout using interval training should be done only once or twice a week with a day off between workouts.

» Check with your doctor first. If you have any medical condition like high blood pressure or asthma, ask your doctor if interval training is safe for you.